Cuba Wanderer

Traveller's Guide to Cuba, not a tourist guide

By Sasha Korniak

First Published by Cuba Wanderer

First Edition

© Copyright Holder Sasha Korniak 2015

All Rights Reserved

www.CubaWanderer.co.uk

ISBN - 978-0993375002

The moral right of the author have been asserted.

British library Cataloguing in Publication Data

A catalogue record for this book is available from the British Library

Library of Congress Cataloguing in Publication Data

A catalogue record for this book is available from the library of Congress

CONTENTS

Why "A Cuba Wanderer" Introduction

The Cuba Wanderer is a Traveller's Guide to Cuba, not a tourist guide and it provides fresh alternative to the mainstream guides. It's written for a new kind of "traveller" who is interested in sharing, exchanging and listening rather than consuming and judging, and it encapsulates a philosophy of peace and sustainable development - either economically, environmentally or socially.

This book came about as a result of my frustration with mainstream guidebooks and poor and misleading travel blogs. I was also disheartened by defamatory organised smear campaigns against the Cuban people and their achievements. To name just a few of these achievements, at the time of writing, 48% of MPs in the National Assembly of People's Power are women. There's also Operation Miracle, which saw over a million cataract operations performed by Cuban doctors for free across the whole of the Caribbean. The 1961 Literacy Campaign resulted in eradicating illiteracy in Cuba in less than a year.

In 1978, the year before I was born, Jorge Dominguez, a Cuban born professor at Harvard University said: "Cuba is a small country, but it has a big country's foreign policy. It has tried to carry out such a policy since the beginning of the revolution, but only in the second half of the 1970s did it have conditions to become a visible and important factor actually shaping the course of events."

In the same year Henry Kissinger, a United States politician, said: "It is time to overcome the ridiculous myth of the invincible Cubans. Whoever heard of Cubans conducting a global foreign policy?"

So let's be clear, Cuban medical programmes alone have reached more people around the world than all of the G8, World Health Organisation and Médecins Sans Frontieres programmes combined, and have been doing so since the early 1970s. This is well documented in Studies of the Americas - Cuban Medical Internationalism by John M. Kirk and H. Michael Erisman and is known throughout the world. However, it is not necessarily reported by Western media.

Cuba trains more doctors from around the world than any other country. ELAM (Latin American School of Medicine) may be the largest and most diverse medical school in the world, with almost 20,000 students attending from around the world and training to be doctors for free. Yes, really, that's seven years of free medical training.

Don't believe it? Listen to Gail Reed talk to T.E.Dx on the internet. http://go.ted.com/bkie

Cubans think, act, feel, care and work differently to anybody I've met in the world and their "Soft Power" diplomacy and humanitarian internationalism is extraordinary and complex. This is summed up best by Fidel Castro. He said: "It lies in the fact that human capital can achieve far more than financial capital. Human capital implies not only knowledge but also crucially important political awareness, ethics, a sense of solidarity, truly human feelings, a spirit of sacrifice, heroism and the capacity to do a lot with very little."

Cuban initiatives have been largely ignored by the West and the Western media, and this continues to be the case – it's not in their best interest to acknowledge them.

I was inspired to write by the Cuban people in Cuba, especially the country's independence leader and national hero Jośe Marti and his work One World, One Nation, Our Americas. I was also influenced by the following women: Celia Sánchez Manduley, Vilma Espín, Haydée Santamaría,Tamara Bunke Bider, better known as "Tania", Anne Frank and Alice Walker, author of the The Color Purple. The Cuban bands Los Van Van and Gente de Zona's, song Bailando is played every minute of the day and helped me along the way.

I also owe a debt to the brilliant Irish author, Dervla Murphy, who has been writing adventure travel books for over 40 years. Her book The Island that Dared: Journeys in Cuba, chronicles a family holiday that the writer took with her daughter and three young granddaughters. It's a little dated now but it's still very informative and relevant.

The Cuba Wanderer is self published, printed on demand therefore better for the environment and able to be updated monthly. Check the web site for events and new information.
www.cubawanderer.co.uk

When to Go Weather Wise

When it gets too hot we suspend all activities and head for the air conditioning, lie on the beach or cool off in the sea. So rather than visiting when it's stifling, it's best to go to Cuba when it's warm or hot and certainly not when it's cold.

While living in Habana in January 2015, I felt it was cold for most of the month and really cold, at 9 degrees Celsius, for about half a week, which was unusual (I was told). 9 degrees Celsius does not sound too bad from the perspective of a person who previously lived in London, but it was still a shock to my system after living in plus 20 degrees Celsius for so long. It affected my fellow Cubans too. On most days in January 2014 and 2015, walking to catch a bus in the early morning for lessons at Habana University, I witnessed the spectacle of Cuban parents ensuring their offspring were suitably dressed for the weather conditions of 10 degrees Celsius, which included scarves, woolly hats and mittens. It was comical to see papas running down the street after their sons or daughters with forgotten scarves or woolly gloves. This is a very serious matter in the eyes of Cuban parents, for it was highly likely that without that warm clothing, their children would freeze to death!

Receiving SMS text messages are free all over the world, so I subscribed to a weather forecast service for Habana, which I also didn't have to pay for. The data originates from the Met Office back in the UK and I intended to use this to plan my week's activities, whether horse riding in Park Lenin or going to the beach. However, the technological advancements behind the term "digital forecasts" clearly have a way to go as my experience was that forecasts for the day ahead were okay, while the forecast for the next day and beyond were useless. I would change my plans to go to the beach as thunderstorms were forecast for much of the week and later experience beautiful skies without a cloud in sight.

Best Months To Go

Oct to Dec - Note: December can be rather wet.

Feb to May - It's dry and warm, increasing in temperature each month.

After May it is really too hot for many travellers - and Cubans too.

Late August until late September is hurricane season but don't worry, Cuba is a world leader in public evacuations and many foreign NGOs use the Cuban model.

Travel Insurance

If you cannot afford travel insurance, then you cannot afford to travel.

People will tell you that it does not matter if you lose luggage because you should be travelling light anyway so that you can afford to replace stuff. Or they'll argue that medical bills in other countries are pretty cheap in the rare event you need a doctor.

Don't listen! Travel insurance is compulsory for all people visiting the island of Cuba.

In most cases, travelling around anywhere in the world will go without any issues or problems. But it does happen. Emergency evacuations and repatriation can cost in excess of $100,000 USD, and hospital costs can run up to thousands of pounds or dollars a day.

Do not travel without insurance and ensure you understand the small print, descriptions of coverage and what you are covered for.

Arriving at Jośe Martí International Airport

Jośe Martí International Airport is the largest and busiest airport, serving several million passengers each year. It is located around 25 km from Habana, Cuba's capital city, near to the town of Boyeros. It is named in the memory of national hero, poet and Cuban patriot Jośe Martí. I have written a chapter about him, which appears later in this book.

Depending on where you're travelling from or the time of year it is, you're going to be warm, hot or even cold! Yes, for half a week in January 2015 I was cold - it was 9°C or 48.2°F. It's highly likely that it is going to be hot, very hot, so if you're going to change into more suitable clothing for the environment I suggest taking them in your hand luggage and getting changed about an hour before landing. Why? You'll see further down the line…

When exiting the aircraft take your time, you are now on an island where "you have to take the time, to take the time."

The reason for my advice on dressing for the weather before you arrive is because at times, but not always, there can big long queues at immigration. In 2014, I left London with my winter coat as it was getting cold and arrived in 25°C/77°F Habana. I was one of the first off the aircraft and then stood for 2 hours in my coat in the queue for immigration as my pockets were full of items I could not fit into my luggage. I then had to collect my other belongings, which included 3 large suitcases and a bike in a box. It's fair to say it got a little warm for me!

Immigration

At the time of writing, when presenting your passport and visa at immigration, you will be asked if you have visited any African counties in the last 30 days. This is due to the Ebola outbreak and the risks posed by yellow fever.

Citizens of the United States still cannot visit Cuba as tourists as this is currently prohibited under US law. Announcements concerning "easing the restrictions" and "new rules" reverberated around the media stratosphere last year and earlier this year. Words or phrases then bounced from our social media walls and then out of our mouths. If you repeat them often enough it becomes the truth, no wait, it becomes politics, or is that religion?

Since January 2015 it no longer necessary for US Citizens to obtain "people-to-people special licenses" as long as their visit is within the scope of 12 categories. Until this time, any US visitors to Cuba were required to apply for a license. But now anyone can go providing they operate within the "rules" and return without any issues. Please find below a link to the US Department of the Treasury, frequently asked questions related to Cuba. http://ow.ly/ROV0O

At the moment they may need to fly through a third country, such as Canada, Mexico or one of the Caribbean islands. Charter flights from the US to Cuba only operate via people-to-people tours. It is best to fly via Cancun in Mexico as the flights are cheap and quick.

Still want to go?

If you want to escape from the US and visit Cuba, which thousands of US citizens do, then you can do this via Canada or Mexico. Simply purchase tickets via Mexican or Canadian travel agents.

OK, purchasing a flight to Cuba from the US can be a little confusing. Online sites such as Orbitz or Kayak do not yet have flights listed to Habana. Presently, due to the US Blockade of Cuba, it may not be possible to book flights to Cuba online with US based travel agents or companies. However, there are other non-US airlines, such as Cubana de Aviación AeroMexico, SunWing, SkyScanner and CubaJet. With Skyscanner (and maybe with other sites) you may need to change the location to display flights to Cuba. Again, this is due to the laws of the US Blockade. For Skyscanner just change the location in the top right corner on the website.

Cubana Airlines	http://ow.ly/ROV7H
Aeromexico	http://ow.ly/ROVa0
SunWing	http://ow.ly/ROVgM
Skyscanner	http://ow.ly/ROViJ
Cubajet	http://ow.ly/ROVoN

Don't forget your visa for Cuba. Visas can be purchased at the airports of connecting countries (such as Mexico City, Cancun,

Toronto or Montreal) for around $25. I also understand that they can be purchased in the US via http://ow.ly/ROVtG

Although "times are a changing" in relation to credit and debit cards from US international banks, cash is king in Cuba. US bank cards will not work in Cuba. Change your US dollars to euros or Canadian dollars before arriving there; this will save you money as there is a surcharge on changing US dollars.

US Travellers can bring back $400 worth of souvenirs, but unfortunately that includes just $100 worth of tobacco and alcohol. (The best rum is the Legendario Elixir de Cuba.)

It's difficult to gauge how long these policies will remain as there might even be changes tomorrow, but don't count on it. Depending on who becomes the next US president there maybe less freedom to visit Cuba for US citizens, so you'd better get a move on!

It you are still worried about encountering questions from US immigration officers upon your return then apply for Global Entry. Global Entry works by simply scanning your passport by computer and then moving you through immigration. Nobody is looking at the stamps and no talking is required. Thousands of people travel to Cuba every year, legally and illegally, and have no issues.

US Passport Holders

Depending on the ever-changing rules within Cuban Immigration, your passport, visa or both will be stamped upon entering the Republic of Cuba. My mother witnessed a US passport holder attempting to stop an immigration officer from doing so by saying, "no no, not my passport" and waving his arms around. The calm and professional female immigration officer replied, "new rule, have a nice day". Don't worry, it is highly unlikely that anything will happen to you upon your return but this could change depending on who wins the future US presidency.

After immigration relax as it can take a little while for luggage to arrive on the carousels. Big items such as bikes and pushchairs will be found at the end of each carousel. There are some VIP lounge services that collect your luggage for you, but I have never experienced these and don't plan to!

After exiting the carousel area you will pass through customs. You should present your completed customs declaration form, which you will have received on the aircraft. You may also be asked to provide your luggage or bag receipt, which should have been stuck to the back of your passport by the check in staff at your departure point.

Customs Regulations

The Cuban Customs or the AGR (Aduana General de la Republica declaration form is easy to complete and, in most if not all of cases, requires hardly any information. Simply fill in your name, nationality, departure point and the names of your family members travelling with you. It is all standard stuff like most other countries in the world. You also have to declare any amount of cash greater than US $5,000.

The following items are not allowed without prior arrangement:

Weapons and ammunition, including knives. Narcotics, live animals, satellite communication equipment, walkie-talkies, vegetables, fruits, and pornography.

I have not experienced any issues with the following: my laptop, professional sound recording equipment, 5 professional microphones, professional HD Camera and video recording equipment devices.

There are some unfounded allegations on the internet regarding restrictions on HD Camera devices and devices with GPS ability, such as phones and cameras. I have taken all these items of equipment into Cuba without any issues.

I would advise practicing caution around taking devices for the solo purpose of triangulating position via GPS (which you may use for going hiking for instance) I'm unaware of the policy, but based on personal experience I suspect these devices might not be allowed. For more information visit the AGR http://ow.ly/ROVGK

Entering The Arrivals Hall

Upon entering the arrivals hall take your time. It will be very busy and you may find it a little intimidating. Remember to relax because "you have the time, to take the time" and you are safe, you are in Cuba!

In the middle of the hall is a bar serving beer, coffee, rum and soft drinks. The toilets are located upstairs. You have time on your hands, you can have a beer and you can people watch. What are you rushing to get to? Also, if there is a queue at the bar or it is closed, there is a snack bar across the road opposite the exit that serves the same items but better coffee.

Top Tip - Before You Leave The Airport

Change your money. I cannot stress too much the importance of changing your money at the airport. There are money exchange offices known as Cadeca (Casa de Cambio) outside on either side of the arrivals hall exits.

Departure Tax

Since March 1 2015, the departure tax of $25 CUC, previously paid by the passenger, has been included in the price of the airline ticket. So now use your $25CUC to buy a bottle of Legendario Elixir de Cuba Rum!

Getting to Habana

Pre-booked OR Pre-arranged Chartered Shuttle Buses & Coaches

Many travellers arriving into the airport will already have had their transfers pre-arranged and paid for in advance by their tour operators. It's easy to find them in the main hall after you pass customs - they will be waiting with signs and displays of your tour operator's logo or your name.

Taxi to Habana

First, don't stress or worry. On exiting the airport via the arrivals hall, state taxis will be located on your left hand side in a big long line - just head to the first in the queue.

Agree the fare first. The rates are pretty fixed from the airport and will set you back around $25CUC or maybe $20CUC if you speak Spanish. The ride from the airport to Habana is around 30 to 40 minutes depending on the time of day and the weather.

For those who are experienced, hardened, wise or on a budget, you might get a much cheaper deal if you head upstairs to the departure floor. Once there go outside and negotiate with the Maquina taxis (Maquinas are pre 1959 North American cars). Also look for Ladas who are dropping passengers off as they should charge less. Aim for around $15CUC.

On the way back to the airport, grab a taxi that is NOT parked outside a hotel, or simply negotiate a rate, again from $15CUC.

By Bus

There are public buses "near" to the airport, but I would not recommend using them if you're laden with luggage.

Although learning to navigate Habana like a local might sound like fun, I'd only recommend it if you speak Spanish. You will also need local national pesos and if it goes wrong you'll need to know how to use the Maquinas.

In the afternoons or evenings you could wait where the taxis load passengers (to the left of the main exit as you walk out) and try to get on one of the long and white bendy buses that run for airport workers. They stop in the middle of the road. Well, they slow down rather than come to a complete standstill. They should follow Boyeros Avenue, better known as Independence Avenue, to the Plaza del la Revolucion (look for the building with the giant face of Che). Get off near or at the Omnibus National Bus Station, where local city buses pass frequently, and then take a Maquina.

The best option is to walk to the bus stop of P12 or P16, which is around 1.5km away. Cubans believe walking more than 2 to 3 blocks is an unimaginable distance so don't believe them if they say it's too far. Turn right out of the arrival hall door and head towards Terminal 2. Both the P12 or P16 will take you to the Plaza del la Revolucion, or if you find it's too far or get lost like I did on my first try, use a Maquina and you are most likely to arrive near to Capitolio.

My mother believes that this route is only for the adventurous traveller. We should all listen to our mothers!

Car Rental

The arrivals hall has several car rental companies, including Rex, Rent a Car, Fenix and Cubanacar. Whatever happens, it is going to be expensive!

My advice is don't drive for long distances at night. Driving is safe in Cuba but could be scary for European or North American drivers at night as the streetlights are very different and car headlights are more powerful than generally allowed in Europe; they can be dazzling for drivers who are unaccustomed to them. I have experienced the odd phenomena on large highways or motorways of feeling that oncoming cars are heading directly towards me, only to find that they are a safe distance away when passing. This is due to the different types of headlight height and positioning of pre-1959 cars and more modern vehicles. It just takes a bit of getting used to. When driving outside of large cities, it's going to be very dark so take care.

Travel Times By Road

Habana Airport to Habana downtown is around 30 to 40 minutes, depending on the time of day and the weather. Habana Airport to Varadero Resorts and Hotels is around 90 minutes to 2 hours, depending on the time of day and the weather.

About the Airport

Terminal 1
Domestic Terminal - Internal flights within Cuba. I have travelled from here to Santiago de Cuba and back.

Terminal 2
US Terminal - Used by flights from and to the United States; a mix of scheduled and charter flights for Cuban Americans and travellers on people-to-people exchange licenses.

Terminal 3
International Terminal - Over 25 international airlines, serving over 60 destinations in more than 30 countries. At this terminal euros are accepted at the bars and cafes.

Terminal 5
Caribbean Terminal - Includes Cuban airlines, AeroCaribbean and Aerotaxi.

Isn't Cuba A Dangerous Country?

In one word, no, Cuba is not a dangerous country. For us in Cuba this question is so funny. Ask people when you are there and see them smile…

Crime levels are low and from my experience take the form of opportunistic theft. This is confirmed by the website of the FCO (Foreign and Commonwealth Office) and other travel guides. Friends of mine have occasionally been targeted by pickpockets' and bag snatchers while visiting tourist sites or nightclubs.

Australians should check out Smartraveller (provided by the Australian government) - http://ow.ly/RGjUF

Canadians should check out http://ow.ly/ROVUH and http://ow.ly/ROW0h

Tourism is the second biggest contributor to Cuba's GDP, so crimes against tourists are punished severely with long prison sentences. I have been told that they are viewed the same as treason - hence the punishment. A Cuban police officer informed me over lunch one day that most reported tourist crimes are solved.

Kidnapping is unheard of in Cuba, unlike other Central and South American countries. When you live in the country you begin to understand that there is no privacy - everybody knows each other. The whole of Cuba has a population of only around 11.5 million, so if anybody commits a crime it's likely to be seen by somebody that recognises or knows them.

It is truly amazing how safe Habana and the rest of Cuba has become since the revolution. As just one example, there are cars called Colectivos and/or Maquinas which operate as taxis and tend to work a specific route (like a bus) around Habana at all times of the day and night. School children, boys and girls from the age of 7 or 8, will take Colectivos across Habana on their own. In other words, every day children get into cars with drivers who are normally a stranger to them and arrive at their destination safely. At night, or more likely in the early hours of the morning, my Cuban and foreign female friends will catch a Colectivo, and are happy to get into them alone. Children walk to and from school in Habana and out in the countryside without incident or in fear.

One of my foreign female friends was picked up by a passing ambulance and driven directly to her door.

My best advice is to just watch out for scams and don't get too drunk. This is the same advice you would be given anywhere else in the world.

A wonderful Irish friend of mine told me about the time a man attempted to snatch her bag. She was so outraged that the whole of Vedado and the rest of Habana could have heard her scream at the thief. He was so intimidated by her reaction that he promptly stopped and returned the bag!

This is not the first time I have heard such a description - so screaming or shouting at the time can stop the thief in their tracks. A few years ago my parents' friends were in a bar in La Habana Vieja (old town). This bar had brilliant live music and people would stand on the street and listen through open windows. My parents' friends witnessed a hand coming through the window from the street, lifting a bag that was on the seat next to its owner who suddenly and loudly leapt onto her chair, pointed at the thief (who by now was holding her bag in mid-air) and screamed at the top of her voice. This not only silenced the playing band but caused the would-be thief to return the bag quickly with an apology – he was desperate to avoid drawing the attention of local Cubans.

Violent crimes happen everywhere in the world but it would be pretty unusual for you to be a victim of this type of crime in Cuba.

Scams

The Salsa Teacher
A lot of Cuban males are teachers of salsa, especially when the foreign woman is pretty and/or blonde.

My Friend Works at The Cigar Factory
Everybody, whether they are a bartender, a guide, a cleaning lady, a taxi driver, a casa owner, or a hotel worker has a father, brother, uncle or friend that works at the cigar factory. These cigars will be

counterfeit (even if they have genuine looking labels or stickers on them) or stolen.

Roadside & Hotel Punctures
Don't let the mechanic take the car alone. The puncture will be repaired but the car might be used as a taxi for most of the day before being returned.

Milk Scams
People might try to tell you that in Cuba milk is only available to tourists, and that they do not have any for their children. This is not true. I have worked in local schools in Vedado, Miramar and central Habana and schoolchildren receive free milk. These scams are very organised and clever. When the scammer has persuaded you to help, they will not take any money directly, but instead take you to a store. Cartons of milk will be removed from the shelves and placed on the checkout, then you will be asked to pay the cashier (I have seen pregnant women used as props by men in these cases). An excuse is made that a brother will collect the cartons later and the cartons remain in the store. After you leave the cartons are returned to the shelf and the money is split between the cashier and your new BFF (Best friend forever).

Money For Medicine
Money for medicine and/or surgery. Cuban healthcare is free for all Cubans and is of a high standard.

Meeting With Jinetero Or Jinetera

This term derives from a Cuban word meaning street jockey. I would describe a jinetero as a hustler, but the word means so much more.

Originally the term jinetero (for men) and jinetera (for women) referred to those associated with prostitution. Today, the meaning is much wider and refers to pretty much all types of swindles.

These will be encountered in tourist areas; outside of these places Cubans will be genuine and honest, so do not prejudge everybody, especially if you have just been walking around Habana Vieja, which is notorious for them.

Now it's all a matter of opportunity, ranging from my "brother" works in a cigar factory, to a smiling stranger approaching you in the street to offer casa particulars (especially if you have luggage with you) or deals on local restaurant or taxis.

Jinterismo is opportunism and while it's not necessarily a criminal activity, the line can get blurred.

Imagine the scenario.

An attractive, muscular Cuban guy says to a Nordic woman, "Hello, do you speak English?"
"Yes, I've been living in London," she replies.
"Oh, great, I am a student of English," grins the Cuban. "Would it be possible to practise my English conversation with you?"
"Sure, I'm happy to help," replies the Nordic lady.
They go to a café or bar where it turns out the guy's English is fluent. But when the bill comes it happens to be twice the normal price, which the Cuban passes to his new friend!
When this happened to me I agreed and suggested we went to the park where it was quieter. Suddenly my Cuban friend was reminded about an appointment they needed to attend and left.

Another example would be for the guy to offer an invitation to dinner in which you pay, then the next night you may see him with another Canadian or European woman.

Now I see that as opportunism rather than criminal activity.

This doesn't just happen in Cuba, it takes place in tourist destinations all over the world, but in Cuba it is conducted with more style and panache.

People have commented to me that in bars and nightclubs Cubans will try to chat them up in order to get free drinks. Well, yes, the same has happened to me, in Cuba and in other countries, but Cubans seem to be judged particularly harshly. It's pretty unfair.

Others have commented about jinetero in terms of the man arranging "girls for prostitution" - now I see this as pure criminality. In my mind there is nothing lower than a man selling others for prostitution. Living in Habana I have encountered these types of individuals over time. Most, if not all, of those known to me have either disappeared from public view due to me introducing them to the criminal justice system or have run in the opposite direction having seen me coming along the street.

You do not need to worry about jinetero/a, just be aware and if it sounds too good to be true, it will be - it's not quantum mechanics.

Personal Items To Take With You

I spent around 4 months reviewing and selecting these items for my personal use in Cuba. Over a year later I have no regrets.

1. Pacsafe TravelSafe 100 Secure Portable Safe

This is brilliant for Cuba and backpackers. The Pacsafe Travel Safe is an anti-theft travel safe, with an exomesh ultimate complete lock and leave system that's slash-proof, snatch-proof and tamperproof. It's designed to stop opportunist theft, and it works! I have had this Pacsafe since 2013 and have used it all over Cuba and the world! It protects belongings that you don't need to carry around. It can hold a volume (approx) of 2.5L/153 inch cubed, weighs 300g-11oz, including the padlock, and its dimensions are 20x35x 1.3cm. See this as a long-term investment. See: http://ow.ly/ROWRU

2. Water Filter bottle

ECO Stainless Pure water filter bottle, 1600 litres

Either buy bottled water every day, which adds an extra $2-$5 to your daily budget, or save money and the environment by buying a bottle with an internal filter.

It works by mouth suction, processing water through a specialised filter that removes waterborne pathogens and reduces chemicals from any fresh water source. I have used water from taps in Hotel, Casa Particulars, lakes and rivers around Cuba with no issues. See: http://ow.ly/ROWTY

3. Ultra light towels

Lightload Towels pack so small that it's pretty amazing when you see the actual size. My advice is to buy the 90x150cm sized ones. See: http://ow.ly/ROWVg

4. Deodorant

The Crystal Deodorant Stick will last months!
See: http://ow.ly/RP8kd

5. Electrolytes, glucose and those minerals!

Sometimes water is not all we need for rehydration, we need other stuff too. These are helpful when you are not used to the environment. See: http://ow.ly/RP8qK

6. SunScreen

Apply P20 once in the morning and that's it, you are protected for up to 10 hours. I'm extremely pale and until I found Riemann P20 I would burn in around 8 minutes. See: http://ow.ly/RP8tM

Cultural Idiosyncrasies in Cuba - Culture & Etiquette

Cubans in Cuba have taught me that my mind was constrained by the way I thought or think. It was limited and programmed. I have been designed to think in a certain way. This effect was from lots of different influences or mechanisms that have been created and now control us.

These mechanisms have been designed or maybe corrupted to serve the interests of just a few. We choose to continue to live this way as we believe there are no other mechanisms to live by as we adjust to live in virtually any situation or condition.

Societies have a elite and they try to stay in power, not only to control the means of production or natural resources, but controlling the way I think and feel. For a long time others have manipulated the way I think, manipulated my thoughts and feelings. Gutenberg's printing press, television and the internet has helped but the elite, governments, finance and media have used these tools to control me further. Living here in Cuba, listening, exchanging and sharing has helped me to understand this, therefore I am trying to be liberated from it.

We are in constant search for something, anything to make us feel better, that could be to look younger, to have status, keeping up with the Jones's, to be an entrepreneur, to be the elite, to be a somebody! Maybe we can find this in the best sports, the best foods or the best clothes, bigger houses, the fastest cars, the best music or best films or glossy magazines, or the best perfume! We can never seem to get enough, consumerism, we are programmed for this and this is reinforced everyday.

So open your feelings and thoughts to a new or different possibility.

Cubans think, act, feel, care and work differently to anybody I've met in the world.

Nearly the whole of the Cuban population believe & feel that they are beautiful, they are not body conscious like the way I have been influenced by distorted images from the television, films, music videos, newspapers, glossy magazines and the internet. After speaking to doctors across the island there is little evidence of eating disorders, like anorexia & bulimia. In Cuba it is popular or fashionable for women of any age, shape or size to wear the tightest clothing possible. Currently for men, bright pink skinny jeans are very desirable to wear, I was confused and asked my Cuban sisters why, "it is like a present we want to unwrap" was the reply! A few years ago it was very fashionable to wear brightly coloured t-shirts, the brighter the better and big buckles for belts and the classic high heels and patterned tights. Today in 2015 it is wedges (shoes) and baseball caps with straight peaks.

In Cuba, we are not exposed to the distorted or photoshopped versions of the impossible look. Dr. Becker, at the Harvard Eating Disorders Centre of Harvard Medical School investigated shifts in body image and eating practices in Fiji over a three-year period. The work began in 1995, one month after satellites began beaming television signals to the region. Fifteen percent in the 1998 survey reported that they had induced vomiting to control their weight researchers said, compared with 3 percent in the 1995 survey and 29 percent scored highly on a test of eating-disorder risk, compared with 13 percent three years before.

Cubans love to pose in front of the camera, pull out yours and they will line up to be photographed regardless of their shape and size.

Cubans like pets. Fish, birds and dogs more than cats it seems, especially huskies, they must be very hot dogs! Dogs in Havana have I.D on their collars, not sure why and better traffic sense than most humans.

Often in parks throughout the island you will see Cubans taking out their finches & budgies for socialising, hanging the bird cages in trees in the parks, so the birds can catch up on the local news and gossip!

There is little use of social media and smartphones but some use of headphones, though people do talk to each other!

Living here I have found that all adults are responsible for the protection of all children. Cuban children are always smiling, happy and well dressed. In the constitution of the republic of Cuba it states that parents are required to love and respect their children and children are required to love and respect their parents! In the 1970s it was entered into the constitution that men must do their fair share of domestic duties, child care and house cleaning! Cuban men will do these duties but will only hang out the washing on a line after dark, as those who do are considered "under the thumb"! In the mornings I witnessed proud fathers walking their children to school, living here I have experienced the very caring relationships and strong family bonds.

Everybody hisses (impossible to express in words) and shouts at one another to attract their attention, small girls have louder voices than grown men! Cubans are very loving & caring to each other, this is shown by how they hold each other when sitting in parks or on the Malecòn. Children are happy & safe to play on the streets with each other. Notice the confidence displayed in the posture of women, they know who is in charge and control.

Cubans have a higher value for "life" that is displayed in the driving around the island and it feels like you are always in shouting distance of a medic.

On passing state taxis say outside a hotel, every single driver will say "Taxi?". Even with 15 taxis in a row, every driver will still ask, just in case you change your mind between the first and the 15th. I have found living here that it took around five and half months before they recognised me and stopped asking. Now they just ask how I'm doing or why I'm still here.

It is fun waiting with excited friends to get the "weekly package", file sharing Cuban style, an external USB hard drive containing around 1TB of music, videos, films, TV shows delivered by a weekly visiting man.

There is no holding back when you like somebody. A few Christmas Eve's ago in a town called Remedios, I was chatting in a circle of a few friends and locals that we just met when more people joined the circle. Unbeknown by me, a local girl swapped places to be next to me. After a few seconds of talking to her what happened next would be best described as like a movie scene from when Dracula attempts to bite a victim on the neck, but in this case she was attempting to kiss me, with me holding her back by her shoulders as I was not sure what was going on. Annoyed, she asked why I was resisting so I replied that I was confused and scared!

Cuban guys have to "catcall" or "comment" when in the vicinity of women, it is like breathing they cannot hold it in! I walked to the University one day behind a young lady heading in the same direction. As we passed guys on the street they catcalled as normal, I remained silent as normal. At the top of the street just before entering the grounds of the campus the young student turned around quickly and grilled me on what was wrong with her and why had I not said anything. Later we met for ice cream as I was intimidated into asking her out.

For the first time in my life I am taller than most at 5'10 and now can see above the crowd at concerts. The music this time was heavy metal so it is not all about the salsa. There were thousands of people there and it was interesting to see how much Cubans enjoy music of any type and cannot help starting to dance, or in this case head banging, at any opportunity when music is playing. They ranged from young teenagers to grandparents, its good to see a 76 year old can still head bang as well as 15 year olds!

I have lost the need for privacy in my life, life in Cuba is very public everybody knows everybody therefore it is very safe.

I can just remember growing up in Europe when we had seasonal vegetables and now here I am eating the last avocado of the season in early November and seeing an abundance of potatoes in March. Most of my food is not found in the "supermarket" but the mercado, where the vegetables are organic not genetically modified, no pesticides are used, so you get better tasting, healthier food.

I have seen changes over time, an increase on the importance of recycling and the reuse of everything. On streets, a man would refill disposable lighters that in other countries would be thrown away, others repair watches, spectacles and shoes, organised now as part of co-operatives.

Street food has been introduced due to the increase of self employed workers as before lunch was provided at work. The new availability of cooking oils has resulted in a taste for anything fried but this has led to an increase of diabetes & hypertension. There has been an increase in the availability of foreign beer, Corona is no longer available replaced by Sol, Heineken has been around for some time and now recently Bavaria and Red Bull have appeared. I will never understand why bottled water is imported from Italy and how they allow Coca-Cola to be served!

Technology has changed with the import of digital cameras and portable speakers, the recent rollout of digital TV and new Wifi hotspots across the island. There is more of everything in the shops, including $900CUC white goods!

There have been further changes regarding the selling of houses and cars, new private enterprises and mass state businesses transferring to co-operatives. I remember the time when the long extension telephone cord was seen in houses being used in the next room to call the boyfriend / girlfriend. Nobody had mobile telephones nor was there any need for them. Most houses have the same make and model stereo hifi throughout the island. I remember when the Government replaced everybody's refrigerators and provided every family with a rice and pressure cooker and then being proudly shown them at every home for months.

Lastly, discovering the best rum by sampling and sharing all of them, frequently, over a long period of time and found it is either Santiago de Cuba or Legendario Elixir de Cuba, but feel I need further time to be sure!

Changing Currency, Money, Getting Cash From Hotels & Banks & The CADECA (Casa De Cambio) Explained

My best advice is to change your money when you arrive at the airport. I understand that some of you may be tired from long flights, but trust me. There are Cadeca (Casa de Cambio) at the airports when you arrive (see my chapter, Arriving at Jose Martí International Airport).

Important note: Hotel rates may not be in your favour.

What Is The CADECA (Casa De Cambio)?

The cadeca is the Cuban government's official money or currency exchange house, where you can exchange most currencies (using credit, debit cards and cash) into Cuban Convertible Pesos (CUC) and exchange CUC into CUP (the National Peso). Look out for the sign displayed outside offices.

It is best to attend a cadeca early or late in the day, preferably Sunday afternoons and never on a Saturday or Monday morning. The process can take anything from 3 minutes to 2 hours - the timescales are unpredictable.

Depending on the office size of the cadeca, there will only be up to 5 people allowed inside at any one time. There will also be a queue – this is normal for Cuba. You may wish you'd gone earlier or decide to come back later - there is always mañana.

When arriving outside the cadeca it might not be obvious who is at the start or front of the said queue, or, more importantly, who is at the back. Now this is may be the one national obsession shared by the British and Cubans - the la cola or queue. I believe that queuing is a national pastime for the British. I witness them joining queues all over the world without necessarily knowing what's at the end of it. It's as if they are just programmed to do so. Cubans, on the other hand, know what's at the end, normally it is ice cream or a bus, but in this case it is the cadeca or bank.

When approaching any queue in Cuba ask in a fairly loud voice "ultimo?" and somebody will either raise their hand, point at somebody or just look blankly at you. If you get the blank look you're at the front and the other people are queuing for the bus. If not, remember the person's face as this is a queue not a line, and take note of the person who appears behind you.

Now this is where the rest of the world can really admire and learn from Cuba. You can actually go off, have a coffee, sit across the road in the shade or do some shopping around the corner, as your position is reserved.

Remember that nine-year-olds, especially nina (girls) have the ability to project their voice or shout louder than most grown men from outside Cuba. I was pretty embarrassed when an eight-year-old girl assisted me in shouting to get the attention of a passing friend, and I know people who would quake in their shoes at the sound of this summons. Until living in Cuba I had never been easily intimidated - it did take some time to get used to.

If you're changing foreign currency you will need your passport or Carne (Cuban ID), but I have not needed ID for changing Convertible Peso to National Peso.

Ensure you dress formally for entering a bank in Cuba; no vests or flips-flops. When inside, the security person (male or female), will direct you to a cash teller. Make sure it's clear how much you want to exchange. If your Spanish is not great then write down the amount before you go.

Banks and cadecas will not accept damaged, spoilt or marked notes or bills. The teller will spend a long time examining each and every note, firstly the front of each note or bill, then the backs and the edges. They will also count the amount of notes or bills a few times (on average around 4 or 5 times).

Depending on which way the wind is blowing, the teller may ask which denominations are preferred. Try not to accept large bills or notes, such as $50 and $100 ones. The highest denomination you want is $20.

For most travellers there are minimal differences between a cadeca and a bank. Banks offer more services, such as stamps for extending your visa. The process for queuing is different in banks. When arriving at the entrance the security person will ask what you require and then ask you to take a seat. Don't worry, they will look after you and indicate when it is your turn. Remember to smile as they are more likely to bump you up the queue.

If you are a Mastercard holder or your cards don't work in the ATM or cashpoint then, in my experience, you'll have more success in banks than in the cadecas. Any unused money can be exchanged back at the airports or donated to myself!

Locations of Cadecas & Banks

Type	Name	Address	Area	City
Casa de Cambio	Direcciòn Territorial Plaza	Calle 12 Entre 21 y 23	Plaza del la Revoluciòn	Habana
Casa de Cambio	Hotel Nacional	Calle O y 21	Plaza del la Revoluciòn	Habana
Casa de Cambio	Hotel Riveria	Calle Paseo - Esq Malecón	Plaza del la Revoluciòn	Habana
Casa de Cambio	Agromercado de 19 y A	Calle 19 es A Vedado	Plaza del la Revoluciòn	Habana
Casa de Cambio	Agromercado 15 y 24	Calle 15 y 24 Vedado	Plaza del la Revoluciòn	Habana
Casa de Cambio	Focsa	Calle M Entre 17 y 19 Vedado	Plaza del la Revoluciòn	Habana
Casa de Cambio	Coppelia Calle L	Calle L Entre 21 y 23	Plaza del la Revoluciòn	Habana
Casa de Cambio	Linea y Paseo	Calle Linea esa a Paseo	Plaza del la Revoluciòn	Habana
Casa de Cambio	Coppelia Parqueo	Calle 23 esq K	Plaza del la Revoluciòn	Habana
Casa de Cambio	Tulipán y Marino	Calle Tulipán esq Marino	Plaza del la Revoluciòn	Habana
Casa de Cambio	17 y K	Calle 17 Entre K y L	Plaza del la Revoluciòn	Habana
Casa de Cambio	26 y 51	Ave 26 esq 51 Neuvo Vedado	Plaza del la Revoluciòn	Habana
Casa de Cambio	17 y G	Calle 17 esq G	Plaza del la Revoluciòn	Habana

Casa de Cambio	Panorama y Tulipán	Calle Panorama esq Tulipán	Plaza del la Revoluciòn	Habana
Casa de Cambio	26 y 41	Ave 26 y 41 Nuevo Vedado	Plaza del la Revoluciòn	Habana
Casa de Cambio	23 y 10	Calle 23 Entre 10 y 12	Plaza del la Revoluciòn	Habana
Casa de Cambio	Arangure n	Ave de Ayestarán y Aranguren	Plaza del la Revoluciòn	Habana
Casa de Cambio	Terminal de Omnibus	Ave de Boyeros y 20 de Mayo	Plaza del la Revoluciòn	Habana
Casa de Cambio	Hotel Vedado	Calle O Entre 23 y 21	Plaza del la Revoluciòn	Habana
Casa de Cambio	Hotel Cohiba	Calle Paseo Entre 1ra y 3ra	Plaza del la Revoluciòn	Habana
Casa de Cambio	Dir Territorial C habana	Belascoain Entre San Nicolás y San Rafael	Centro Habana	Habana
Casa de Cambio	Carlos III	Ave de Carlos 3 esa A marques González	Centro Habana	Habana
Casa de Cambio	Zanja	Calle Zanja esa Soledad	Centro Habana	Habana
Casa de Cambio	Neptuno y Consulado	Calle Neptuno esq Consulado	Centro Habana	Habana
Casa de Cambio	Chávez y Tetuán	Calle Jon de tetuán esa Chávez	Centro Habana	Habana
Casa de Cambio	Infanta y Estrella	Ave de Infanta esq Estrella	Centro Habana	Habana

Casa de Cambio	Fin de siglo	Boulevard de San Rafeal	Centro Habana	Habana
Casa de Cambio	Direcciòn Territorial Plaza	Calle Monte y Cristina	Habana Vejia	Habana
Casa de Cambio	Lonja del Comercio	Calle Oficios esq Baratillo	Habana Vejia	Habana
Casa de Cambio	Egido	Calle Egido Entre Gloria y Monserrate	Habana Vejia	Habana
Casa de Cambio	Obispo	Calle Obispo esq Compostela	Habana Vejia	Habana
Casa de Cambio	Hotel Sevilla	Paseo del Prado esq Refugio	Habana Vejia	Habana
Casa de Cambio	Obispo 257	Calle Obispo No 257	Habana Vejia	Habana
Casa de Cambio	La Isla de Cuba	Calle monte entre Aponte y Cienfuegos	Habana Vejia	Habana
Banks	23 y 8	Calle 23 esq 8	Plaza del la Revoluciòn	Habana
Banks	26 y 37	Calle 26 esq 27 Nuevo Vedado	Plaza del la Revoluciòn	Habana
Banks	Caja d Ahorro	Loma y Tulipán	Plaza del la Revoluciòn	Habana
Banks	Mitrans	Ave Carlos M de Céspedes esq Tulipán	Plaza del la Revoluciòn	Habana
Banks	23 y M Sánchez	Calle 23 No 1054 esq Montero Sánchez	Plaza del la Revoluciòn	Habana

Banks	Focsa	Calle 17 No 55 Entre M y N	Plaza del la Revoluciòn	Habana
Banks	San Lázaro y N	San Lázaro No 1158 esq N	Plaza del la Revoluciòn	Habana
Banks	Linea y Paseo	Linea No 705 Entre Paseo y A	Plaza del la Revoluciòn	Habana
Banks	Conesjo de Estado	Carlos Manuel de Céspedes y Colòn	Plaza del la Revoluciòn	Habana
Banks	La Rampa	23 No 74 Entre P y Malecòn La Rampa	Plaza del la Revoluciòn	Habana
Banks	Linea y M	Linea y M	Plaza del la Revoluciòn	Habana
Banks	MINREX	MinREX	Plaza del la Revoluciòn	Habana
Banks	Monte y Carmen	Máximo Gòmez No 702 esq Carmen	Habana Vieja	Habana
Banks	Empedra do y Aguiar	Empedrado esq Aguiar	Habana Vieja	Habana
Banks	O'Reilly esq Compostela	O'reilly No 402 esq Compostela	Habana Vieja	Habana
Banks	Prado y Animas	Prado No 307 Entre Animas y Virtudes	Habana Vieja	Habana
Banks	San José y Monserrate	San José y Monserrate	Habana Vieja	Habana

Denominations & Lingo - Currency, Cash, Money

Cuba has two currencies, which is fascinating for a few days. The National Peso, written as CUP, and the Convertible Peso, written as CUC and known locally as the kook or dollar.

There are plans to change to one currency and the first part of this process started on the 1st February 2015 with the issuing of new, higher denomination National Peso notes. Arrangements have been made for all establishments to accept them. Previously some shops would only accept Convertible Pesos - known locally as dollar stores. There are no timescales on how long the transition will take so right now it's important to know the difference between them, and how to exchange Convertible Pesos to National Pesos.

On the street in Cuba, the word "pesos" can refer to both the National Peso and the Convertible Peso, which means it can get confusing.

One Convertible Peso is worth, or can be exchanged for, 24 National Pesos. This does not remove the confusion for tourists as Convertible Pesos can be, but not always, referred to as dollars.

Don't worry, within a few hours or days you should be a pro.

The colour and images on Convertibles Peso banknotes are very different to the National Peso, and they have "Pesos Convertibles" clearly written in the centre.

For first time travellers one way to tell the difference is to look at the images on them - Convertible Pesos have pictures of monuments on the front and National Pesos have pictures of faces.

There are denominations of 100, 50, 20, 10, 5, 3 and 1.

Before arriving in Cuba, US travellers should exchange USD dollars for any other currency. Euros are best, but so are Canadian dollars and British Sterling Pounds. (No, these notes are not referred to as Queen Elizabeth's money and no, I don't know HRH either!). In Cuba, USD dollar exchanges are taxed between 12-20%.

Credit Cards, Debit Cards & ATMs

Although "times are a changing" in relation to credit and debit cards from US international banks, cash is king. US bank cards will not work in Cuba.

Credit cards - Non US-based bank card holders will generally be able to use credit cards in upmarket hotels.

Debit Cards – Again, those with cards from non US-based banks will be able to use them at ATMs. From experience, some European MasterCard holders have encountered issues and have had to go inside the banks or cadecas to withdraw cash.

Visa Debit is a better experience. Maestro is from MasterCard but depending on the issuing country, they can work. Not all banks are the same. My HSBC card from the United Kingdom works in Cuba, but my Turkish friend's HSBC card doesn't.

Two fellow students from Germany did have this difficulty for 4 days in a row, with the cashier just stating "transaction declined". In Cuba, it is normal for explanations to have little or no meaning. For example, "Can you tell me why the transaction was declined" - Answer "Porque", which in English is "because". Don't worry, you'll get used to this after time. While it may appear to many travellers as rudeness, I can assure you this is not the Cuban people's intention.

I have experienced ATMs stating "Transaction Cancelled" after successfully withdrawing cash - but sadly have still been charged.

Sometimes ATMs just display "transaction declined" for no reason. ATMs in Cuba also tend not to dispense cash between Sunday afternoon and Monday morning. I thought this was to do with Sunday "being a day of rest", but it is more to do with my UK-based bank not being available internationally on a Sunday evening. You need to remember that you may be in a different time zone to your bank.

To be very clear, currently no cards issued by a US bank inside or outside the US are accepted in Cuba. This includes American Express, Diners Club and your Starbucks loyalty card. Incidentally, there are no Starbucks in Cuba and we all hope there never will be because Cuban coffee is so much better.

Charges vary from bank to bank, country to country, even account to account with the same bank. You need to check with your own and keep all ATM receipts - not because of banking issues, but because it helps with insurance claims if your cash is lost or stolen.

TOP TIP

Today, fraud prevention in banks is very sophisticated. I would advise you to inform your bank of your holiday destination and dates of travel, and then update them with your mobile telephone number. My banks, HSBC and Lloyds, send me a SMS text message to confirm the transaction was made by me. So take your mobile with you when going to the ATM or cashpoint.

Tourist Information Offices

Infotur - Can be the best place for info, if you try!

Here, teams of well-informed professionals with a lot of local and national knowledge and different languages will offer you free and accurate information most days of the year. The quality of the information depends how they have been treated by others before your turn, and how you treat them. See their web site for more details http://ow.ly/ROW66

Some of the offices will offer the following and some will not:
- Information on Cuban tourist services, events and places.
- Specialised programmes and promotional brochures, especially in Baracoa!
- Maps, guides, posters and postcards.
- Phonecards, movies, CDs and Cuban music.
- Magazines, newspapers, books and promotional videos.
- Reservation services, tours, trips, walks and car rentals. This does happen in the city office of Santiago de Cuba. You can book a coach to Baracoa from this office and the pick up point is just outside too, saving you from returning to the Viazul bus station.
- Photocopying and printing services.
- Transmission of fax and emails.

Locations

Infortur -	Location	Address	Tele	Email
Airport	Jośe Martí International al Airport	Terminal 2	53 7 642101	aerodir@enet.cu
Havavna	Havana Vieja	Obispo No 524 Between Bernaza Y Villegas	53 7 863 6884	infotur@hvieja.info tur.cu
Havavna	Havavna	Quitrín Obispo Y San Ingacio	53 7 866 3333	infotur@hvieja.info tur.cu
Havana	Playas Del Este	Ave 5ta between 468 y 470. Guanaco.	53 7 796 6868	infogua@enet.cu
Havana	Playas Del Este	Ave Las Terrasas y Calle 10, Santa María del Mar	53 7 796 1111	infoeste@enet.cu
Havana	Playa	Ave 5ta y 112. Miramar.	53 7 204 7036	infoplaya@habana .infotur.cu
Pinar Del Río	Hotel Vueltabajo	Calle Martí #103 Esq. Rafael Morales	53 48 75 4803	infotur@minturpr.c o.cu
Viñales	Calle Salvador	Cisneros # 63B, Viñales	53 48 796263	infopinr@enet.cu

Varadero	Aeropuerto			
Varadero		1ra Ave Calle 13	53 45 667044	vardirec@enet.cu
Varadero	Centro Comercial Hicacos	1ra Ave Between 46 y 47	53 45 66 2961	vardirec@enet.cu
Cienfuegos	Delegación MINTUR	Calle 37 #1406 between 14 y 16 Punta Gorda	53 43 51 4653	infocfgo@enet.cu
Villa Clara	Aeropuerto Intenraiton al Abel Santamiría			
Villa Clara	Calle Cuba No 68 entre Candelaria y e. Machado	Santa Clara	53 42 22 7557	director@inforturvlc.tur.cu
Ciego De Ávila	Aeropuerto International Jardines del Rey, Cayo Coco			
Ciego De Ávila	Calle Honorado del Castillo, Edificio 12 Plantas		5333 209109	infotur @ciegoavila.infotur.cu
Trinidad	Plaza Santa Ana	Calle Santo Domingo	53 41 99 8257	infotri@enet.cu
Camagüey	Aeropuerto International		53 32 26 5807	infocmg@enet.cu

	al Ignacio Agramonte			
Camagù ey	Plaza de les Trabajador es Ignacio Agramonte	No 448 Entre López Recio y Charles A Dana	53 32 256794	infocmg@enet.cu
Las Tunas	Hotel Las Tunas	Ave 2 de Deicmbre	5331 372717	infotunas@infotun as.co.cu
Holguín	Infotur Aeropuerto Internation al Frank Pais			holgdir@enet.Cu
Holguín	Edif Pico Cristal 2do piso calle Martí Libertad		53 24 425013	holgdir@enet.Cu
Granma	Aeropuerto Internation al Sierra Maestra			
Granma	Centro Comercial Telégrafo	Calle Saco Entre Mármol y Martí. Bayamo	5323 42 2599	infogran@enet.cu
Santiago de Cuba	Aeropuerto Internation al Antonio Maceo			
Santiago de Cuba	Parque Céspedes		53226694 01	infostgo@enet.cu

	Lacret 701 Heredia			
Guntána mo	Calle Anonio Maceo No 192 A Entre Maravi y Frank pais, Baracoa		53 21 64 1871	infogtmo@enet.cu
Guntána mo	Hotel Guantánom o - Ahogados y 13 Norte		53 21 64 1872	infogtmo@enet.cu

Important Numbers & Emergency Assistance

Medical Emergency	106
Police	113
Fire	105

Help and assistance is available in Cuba, if you know about it. It amazes me how many people don't know about Asistur. If you run out of cash while you are staying in Cuba or you have found that your cards don't work, Asistur will take care of your financial emergency. They will provide money in exchange for cash deposited from a relative or friend abroad. They charge around 10% for these requested amounts plus 17.00 CUC to cover banking costs. The steps in arranging this are too complex to explain here as different countries have different rules.

Phone them on (53 7) 861 8920, visit their offices or send an to e-mail asistenciafinanciera@asistur.cu http://ow.ly/ROWc9

Australians can also use their consular service (see below).
http://ow.ly/ROW8h
24-hour Consular Emergency Centre +61 2 6261 3305 or 1300 555 135 or SMS +61 421 269 080
http://ow.ly/ROW9O

Asistur Medical Assistance

- Outpatient medical care in hospital.
- Monitoring of patient's condition.
- Obtaining and sending of medical reports.
- Coordination of wheelchairs and medication, air and land ambulance services and coordination of medical expenses with your insurer.
- Reception and accommodation for foreign doctors and paramedics. Authorisation for air ambulance landings, coordination of air and land ambulance services, assistance to air ambulance crew.

Other services

- Retrieval of misplaced luggage/bags.
- Coordination of new travel documents, legal assistance and payment of bail bond.
- Insurance products for foreign people with temporary residence in the Republic of Cuba (like me!) Health cover is calculated according to the age and gender of the person.

Offices - Asistur

Mondays to Fridays, 9:00am-3:00pm

Habana
Calle Prado No. 208 entre Trocadero y Colón
Tel:(537) 866 4499
Fax: (53 7) 866 8087
Email: asisten@asistur.cu

Matanzas (Varadero)
Calle 30 y 1ra. Ave. No. 103
Telefax: (53 45) 66-7277
Email: asisturvaradero@enet.cu

Ciego de Avila
Villa Azul
Bloque 15 Apto 250
Carretera a Cayo Guillermo Km 1 y ½
Cayo Coco
Telefax: (53 33) 30-8150

Holguin
Hotel Pernik (lobby)
Avenida Jorge Dimitrov y
Plaza de la Revolucìon
Ciudad Holguin
Telefax: (53 24) 47-1580

Santiago de Cuba
Hotel Casagranda, Calle Heredia No. 201
entre San Felix y
San Pedro
(frente al Parque Céspedes)
Telefax: (53 22) 68-6128

HOSPITALS ASISTUR SERVIMED

Clinics or Hospitals that assist tourists are called SERVIMED. These provide emergency medical care and are located in most major tourist areas around the island.

Habana
Centro Internacional "Camilo Cienfuegos" -
well known for its good pharmacy.
Calle L No. 151 and calle 13
Vedado. Ciudad de La Habana
Tel: (53 7) 32-5554 > 32-5555 > 32-5597
Fax: (53 7) 33-3536 > 33-3578
Email: cirpcc@infomed.sld.cu

Hospital Nacional Hermanos Amejeiras
San Làzaro No 701, Centro Habana
You need to enter via the lower level off Padre Varela.
Tel: 877 6053

The Círa García Hospital - Clínica Círa García,
Calle 20 No. 4191, corner of Street Av. 41 and Playa
Tel: 204-2668 or 204-2489

Habana Pharmacies
Hotel Habana Libre,
831 9538 - Calle L - between Calle 23 and 25 Vedado

Varadero
Clinica Internacional de Varadero
Calle 61 y 1ra, Varadero. Matanzas
Telefonos: (53 5) 66-7710 Fax: (53 5) 66-7226
Email: clinica@clinica.var.cyt.cu

Cienfuegos
Clinica Internacional de Cienfuegos
Calle 37 No. 202 e/ 2 y 4
Punta Gorda. Cienfuegos
Tel: (53 432) 45-1622 > 45-1623

Cienfuegos
Clinica Internacional de Cienfuegos
Calle 37 No. 202 e/ 2 y 4
Punta Gorda. Cienfuegos
Tel: (53 432) 45-1622 > 45-1623

Trindad
Clinica Internacional de Trinidad
Calle Lino Perez No. 130 esq. Reforma
Trinidad. Sancti Spiritus
Tel: (53 419) 3391

Cayo Coco
Clinica Internacional de Cayo Coco
Hotel Tryp Club Cayo Coco. Ciego de Avila
Tel: (53 33) 301205 > 301300

Camaguey
Clinica Internacional de Santa Lucia
Residencia No. 4, Playa Santa Lucia. Camaguey
Tel: (53 32) 366203
Fax: (53 32) 365300

Holguin
Clinica Internacional de Guardalavaca
Calle 2da s/n
Playa Guardalavaca. Holguin
Tel: (53 24) 3-0291

Santiago de Cuba
Clinica Internacional Santiago de Cuba
Calle 13 y 145
Reparto Vista Alegre. Santiago de Cuba
Tel: (53 226) 42589 Fax: (53 226) 87001

Consulates and Embassies

Angolan Embassy in Cuba	5ta. Ave. No. 1012, e/ 10 y 12, Miramar, Playa, Havana, Cuba	Phone (+53) 7 204 4391, (+53) 7 204 4392	Fax (+53) 7 204 0487, (+53) 7 204 4390
Argentinian Embassy in Cuba	Calle 36 No. 511 Entre 5ta y 7ma, Miramar, Playa, 11300 Havana, Cuba	Phone 005372042565 005372042972 005372042110	Fax (+53) 7 204-2140
Austrian Embassy in Cuba	Avenida 5ta A No. 6617, esq. a calle 7, Miramar, Havana, Cuba	Phone (+53) (7) 204 28 25	Fax (+53) (7) 204 12 35
Belgian Embassy in Cuba	Calle 8 no 309/3ra y 5ta Ave., Miramar Playa , Havana, Cuba	Phone (+53) (7) 204.24.10, (+53) (7) 204.25.61	Fax (+53) (7) 204.48.06
Bulgarian Embassy in Cuba	Calle "B" 252, Entre 11 y 13, Vedado, Ciudad de La Habana 10400, Cuba	Phone +53 7 833 31 25, +53 7 833 31 26	
Canadian Embassy in Cuba	Calle 30, No. 518 esquina a 7ma, Miramar, Havana, Cuba	Phone (53-7) 204-2516	Fax (53-7) 204-2044

Canadian Consulate in Cuba	Calle 13 e/Avenida Primera y Camino del Mar, Varadero, Matanzas, Cuba	Phone 53 (45) 61-2078	Fax 53 (45) 66-7395
Canadian Consulate in Cuba	Hotel Atlantico, Suite 1, Guardalavaca, Holguín, Cuba	Phone (53-24) 430-320	Fax (53-24) 430-321
Chinese Embassy in Havana, Cuba	Calle 13, #551, Entre Cyd, Vedado, Ciudad de la Habana, Republica de Cuba	Phone 0053-7-8333005	Fax 0053-7-8333092
Czech Embassy in Havana, Cuba	Ave. Kohly No. 259 entre 41 y 43 , Nuevo Vedado , Ciudad de La Habana , C.P. 10600, CUBA	Phone (++53-7) 8833201	Fax (++53-7) 8833596
Danish Consulate in Havana, Cuba	Paseo de Marti (Prado) 20, Piso 4, Apt. 4 B Zona 2, 10200 Havana, Cuba	Phone +53 (7) 8668 128 + 53 (7) 8668 144	Fax +53 (7) 8668 127
Egyptian Embassy in Havana, Cuba	5 TA AVENIDA NO. 1801, ESQ. A 18, MIRAMAR	Phone (537) 242542 - 242441	Fax (537)240905

Ethiopian Embassy in Havana, Cuba	5ta Ave. No. 6604 , apto 3 e/66 y 68 Miramar, Havana, Cuba	Phone 0053 7 206 9905	Fax 0053 7 206 9907

Finnish Consulate in Havana, Cuba	Calle 21-A y23, Cubanacan, La Habana	Phone +53-7- 2040 793	Fax +53-7- 2040 793

French Embassy in Havana, Cuba	Calle 14 - NR 312, entre 3RA y 5TA, Miramar Playa	Phone (00 537) 201 31 31	Fax (00 537) 201 31 07

French Consulate in Havana, Cuba	Calle 14 - n' 312, entre 3RA y 5TA, Miramar Playa	Phone [53] (7) 20 13 131	Fax [53] (7) 20 13 127

German Embassy in La Habana, Cuba, Cuba	Calle 13, No. 652, Esquina á B, Vedado, La Habana., P.O Box 6610, La Habana, Cuba.	Phone (0053 7) 833 24 60 / (0053 7) 833 25 39	Fax (0053 7) 833 15 86

Italian Embassy in Havana, Cuba	5 Avenida n. 402, Esquina Calle 4, Miramar	Phone 53 7 204 5615	Fax 53 7 204 5659

Mexican Embassy in Province City Of Havana, Cuba	Street 12 No. 518, Esq. 7ma. Avenue, Miramar Distribution, Municipality Beach	Phone (537) 204-7722 al 25, 204-2498, 204-2553, 204-2583	Fax (537) 204-2717

Mozambican Embassy in Havana, Cuba	Ave. 7a No. 2203, Miramar, Havana, Cuba	Phone (+53-7) 2042445, 2042443	Fax (+53-7) 2042232

Dutch Consulate in Havana, Cuba	Calle 8, No 307, Entre 3ra y 5ta Ave Miramar, Havanna, Cuba	Phone 00-53-7-2042511	Fax 00-53-7-2042059

Norwegian Embassy in Havana, Cuba	Calle 30 #315, e/3ra y 5ta Avenida, Miramar, Playa Ciudad	Phone +53-7-204-0696 or 204-4410 or 204-4411	Fax +53-7-204-0699

Palestinian Embassy in Havana, Cuba	Calle 20 No. 714 Entre 7Ma, Y.9 NA Miramar	Phone 537-242556 Res: 537-241114	Fax 537-241159

Polish Consulate in Havana, Cuba	Calle G no.452 esq. 19, Vedado, PO Box 6650	Phone (+53-7) 662439-40	Fax (+53-7) 662442

Portuguese Embassy in Cuidad Havana, Cuba	Av. 7ª nº 2207 Esq. 24 Miramar	Phone +53.7.204.0149	Fax +53.7.204.2593

Romanian Embassy in Havana, Cuba	Calle 21, no. 307 entre H e I,, Vedado, La Habana	Phone (00) (53) (7) 333322 or (00) (53) (7) 333325	Fax (00) (53) (7) 333324

Russian Embassy in Havana, Cuba	5-a Avenue, N 6402, between 62 and 66, Miramar	Phone (+537) 204-10-85, 204-26-86, 204-26-28, 204-10-80	Fax (+537) 204-10-38

Slovak Embassy in Miramar-Playa Havana, Cuba	Calle 66, No. 521, Entre 5ta B y 7ma	Phone (+53-7) 2041884/+53-7-2041885	Fax (+53-7) 2041883

South African Embassy in 5ta. Ave. No.4201 Esq. 42, Cuba	5ta. Ave. No.4201 esq. 42 , Miramar Playa Ciudad de La Habana	Phone + 537 204 9671,+ 537 204 9676	Fax +53-7-2041101

Spanish Embassy in Havana, Cuba	Calle Corcel, 51 (esquina a Zulueta) , Apartado Postal: 845, Havana 10100 Cuba	Phone (+53) 7 866 80 25 / 26 / 31 (+53) 7 866 02 50 / 51	Fax (+53) 7 866 80 06

Swedish Embassy in Havana, Cuba	Calle 34, No 510, entre 5 y 7 ave., Miramar, Havanna, Cuba	Phone (+53) 7 204 28 31	Fax (+53) 7 204 11 94

Swiss Embassy in Havana, Cuba	5ta Avenida no. 2005, entre 20 y 22 Apartado postal 60, Miramar Ciudad de la Habana 11300 Cuba	Phone (+53) 7 204 26 11	Fax (+53) 7 204 11 48

Turkish Embassy in Havana, Cuba	5 Ta Avenida no 3805, Entre 36 y 40 Miramar, Ciudad	Phone +1 – 613 – 902 – 57 11	Fax 00 537 204 28 99
British Embassy in Havana, Cuba	Calle 34 no. 702 esq 7ma , La Habana, Cuba	Phone +537 214 2200	Fax +537 214 2218
US Embassy in Havana, Cuba	Calzada between L & M Streets, Vedado, Havana	(53)(7) 839-4100 (+53)(7)-831-4100	

Electricity

The electricity supply in Cuba is an interesting mix of 110v/60Hz, 220V and maybe something in between. Both the flat 2 pin and round 2 pin plugs are used.

Before travelling to Cuba buy a Surge Protected Worldwide Travel Adapter with a 6A Fuse. These types of devices or adapters do not convert voltage. You can buy these online or at the airport, at a cost of around £11.99/€16.86/US$18.72/CAD$23.57/AUD$24.92

Surge protection shields your electrical equipment from damaging spikes whilst travelling. (Spikes and brown outs are common in Cuba.) Most come with built-in 6A fuses, safety shutters, AC 110 or 240V inputs and adapters for the UK, Europe, Americas, Japan and Australia.

As I am living here and not just visiting I have experienced many different situations with power. On the whole there are few problems, but I would advise not to leave electrical devices plugged in and then left unattended. Additionally, I would not charge laptops or similar devices or watch TV during electrical storms as most buildings don't have lightning protection.

There are power cuts, not black outs. Power cuts are isolated to local apartments, blocks or areas and last between 1 minute and a few hours. Blackouts would cover a whole city, which has not happened for a few years.

TOP TIP

Showers

It is normal for some showers in Cuba to have electrical cabling on display leading from the showerhead to a fuse breaker. It is usual for sparks, accompanied by loud noises, or a type of electrical arcing to happen when using switches located on the top of the showerhead. Don't worry! This is normal for Cuba. It adds to the sense of adventure and nothing has happened to me or anyone I know – yet! More people slip in the shower while worrying about the electrical cabling!

Visa & Extensions

Tourist Visa (Tourist Card)

The Tourist Visa or Tourist Card is only for the purposes of tourism.

For most of the world, it is valid for one single entrance into Cuba for a 30-day trip and can be extended for an additional 30. Lucky holders of Canadian passports have visas that are valid for 90 days and can be extended for an additional 90.

Minors must have their own Tourist Card even if they are travelling under their parent's passport.

To obtain a visa in person at a consulate, the following documents are needed:
- A valid passport
- A plane ticket detailing entry and return dates
- Travel insurance
- A photocopy of your passport
- A completed application form
- Payment of the consular fee for this service £15 in the United Kingdom. (Personal cheques are not accepted! Other options

are cash, postal orders and banker's drafts payable to HAVIN BANK are accepted.)

The follow items are needed to obtain a visa by mail:

- A legible photocopy of valid passport
- A legible photocopy of plane ticket detailing entry and return dates
- Payment of the consular fee for this service either postal order or banker's drafts payable to HAVIN BANK.
- Stamped self-addressed envelope for the visa to be sent back

If the application is made by mail or via a third party, an extra consular fee will be charged. (In the UK £19) When obtaining a visa in person, all payments must be made in cash or, postal orders and banker's drafts. All cash sent by mail will be refused and returned at the risk of the applicant.

TOP TIP

Travellers from the United Kingdom should be aware of the Cuban Visa Scam.

If in the UK, ensure that you are using the correct website for the Cuban Embassy.

http://www.cubadiplomatica.cu/reinounido/EN/Mission/Consula rSectioninUnitedKingdom.aspx

The following claims to be the website (without stating it), but really it's just a third party agent that charges you more for a service you can do yourself. The website is http://cuba.embassyhomepage.com

Most tour operators or airlines should be able to offer assistance in obtaining a tourist visa.

In most countries, tourist visas are issued by tour/travel companies. Alternatively, they are available via the Cuba consular services in your country. Visas can also be purchased at the airports of connecting countries (such as Mexico City, Cancun, Toronto or Montreal) for around $25. I also understand that they can be purchased in the US via http://ow.ly/ROVtG

Extending Your Visa

You can only extend your visa when you have between 3 and 5 days left, so be careful if your last day is a Sunday (although I have heard that some immigration offices are open at the weekend). Dervla Murphy, author of The Island that Dared: Journeys in Cuba also wrote about falling foul of the process.

Remember to print out all your paperwork before arriving in Cuba and also photocopy your passport. If you wish to print after you arrive this may take a whole day. In theory, you will need the following:

- Payment Stamps
- Receipt for the Stamps
- Current Visa
- Passport
- Proof of travel insurance
- Proof of return flight ticket
- Proof of residency in a casa particular or hotel on the day of your extension application.

Stamps

Payment for extending your visa is made with stamps, to the value of 25CUC, which can be obtained from banks across the island. Payment cannot be made at immigration offices. You can purchase the stamps in any city - not just where you are extending your visa.

Receipt For Stamps

Due to counterfeiting and the use of stolen stamps it is recommended that you retain your stamp receipt as proof of purchase. At my last visa extension, the immigration officer didn't even take one look at the receipt before screwing it up and tossing it into the bin, but on other occasions it has been vigorously scrutinised.

I also recommend making a note of all casa particulars or hotels stayed in over the last 30 days, including names, addresses and telephone numbers. There is no immigration requirement to do this but based on my experience it does make the process smoother.

Business Card Of Current Casa Particular

At most casa particulars, the owners will have business cards, and these are very helpful with the immigration process. There is an immigration requirement for you to be registered at a casa particular or hotel on the day of your visa extension.

I have heard in the past about needing a casa receipt as part of the immigration process, but I've never actually been given one of these receipts and have always just used the business card. If not, I just write down the details of the casa particular, including its name, address and telephone number.

Current Visa

You will need to take your current visa with you to the immigration office as the extension will be glued to the back of it. This will be checked when you leave the airport. There are fines for non-compliance of around $100 CUC per day.

Passport

You would be surprised how many people actually forget to take their passport.

In certain areas of Habana, when registering at a casa particular, the owner is required to register you with the immigration service the following day with your visa. This is fairly typical in central Habana and therefore you need to time the extension of your visa carefully.

Travel Insurance

You will need documented proof of travel insurance from day one when you arrive in Cuba. This trips up a lot of tourists and travellers when applying for an extension. You will need proof that you have purchased travel insurance for the full duration of your stay. I have heard that showing a credit card works too.

Return Flight

Most tickets are electronic E-tickets, but many airlines will send an email confirming your arrival and departure dates. Print this out before leaving for Cuba.

Top Tip

Print out all your paperwork before you leave for Cuba as getting documents printed or copied after you arrive requires planning and possibly a whole morning or afternoon (unless you already know somewhere to get it done).

All the dates will need to match and the immigration officer is likely to repeat his or her questions. This won't necessarily be to do with you, it's more about officers ensuring their work is correct and precise. Whatever work they do, Cubans take a lot of pride in it.

Most towns or cities have immigration offices check with your casa owners for the address.

Business Hours, Trading Times & National Holidays

It is traditional in Cuba to get tasks or errands done early in the morning when it's cooler, therefore you need to rise early with the sun.

Business meetings, education lectures, presentations, conferences, medical appointments and work appointments all happen mainly in the morning. From my experience appointments and meetings arranged for the afternoon tend not to happen.

Banks & The Cadecas

Plan ahead and get there early in the morning.

Banks open around 8am and 9am and close between 3pm and 7pm, depending on the branch or type of bank. Some banks are not open on Sundays and close early on Wednesdays and Saturdays.

Cadeca (Casa de Cambio) open at 9pm and close, depending on the branch, at around 7pm. The Cadeca are similar to the banks and normally open on Sundays (but they do close early on the weekends).

Shops

Most shops are open for 12 hours a day, depending on the type and location. They usually open between 8:30am and 9am and close at either 8.30pm or 9pm. There are some small convenience stores that open 24/7.

National Holidays

1st January	Liberation Day
2nd January	Victory of the Armed Forces Day
1st May	Labour Day - Mayday International Workers' Day
25th-27th July	National Rebellion Celebration
28th September	Festival for the CDR
10th October	Anniversary of the 1868 War of Independence
17th November	International Students' Day
27th November	Anniversary of the execution of eight medical
17th December	Freedom of the Cuban five arrived back in Habana
25th December	Christmas Day

Children's Day

The third Sunday in July is "Children's Day" in Cuba. This provides children and adolescents with a special day of celebration and it takes place in streets and parks and in recreational and cultural centres. It is brilliant to explore parks on this day and watch local life.

Students' day

Students' Day takes place on 17th November when the nation celebrates past and present student struggles around the globe. The date was selected to pay tribute to the resistance carried out by students in Prague against the Nazi invasion in 1939.

On this day, Czechoslovakian students decided to fight for their nation´s freedom and carried out a heroic clash in Prague against the fascism that was invading their country. The Nazi invading forces fired upon them, killing many and sending survivors to a concentration camp.

In my experience, the opinions of students in Cuba are regarded as extremely important. Students of all ages have representation at the National Assembly of Cuba.

Medical Students Executed November 1871

On 25th November 1871, the Spanish Governor of Habana arrested eight medical students at their school. This took place during the Ten Years' War - or the Guerra de los Diez Años - which was Cuba's fight for independence from Spain. The students were accused of desecrating the tombstone of a Spaniard, which wasn't true.

The following day, the eight young students, who were aged between 16 and 21, were tried by the order of an acting Captain General in the absence of the General Count of Balmaseda of Cuba. The first trial wasn't accepted by a group of pro Spanish volunteers who had assembled in front of the building where the trial was held. So the students were tried again and subsequently condemned to death by firing squad.

When the General of Cuba returned to Habana he did not impose a lower sentence. Just two days after their arrest all 8 students were executed. This date (27th November) is commemorated as a national day of mourning.

Students in Habana will never forget the names of the eight young people or what happened to them. Every year they march from the steps of Habana University to remember Alonso, Anacleto, José, Ángel, Juan, Carlos Torre, Eladio, and Carlos Verdugo

27th Jan - Outside Habana University - Light Parade

On 27th January, university students, especially students like myself who attend the University of Habana, recognise and celebrate the historical tradition of their generation and of those before them during a ceremony of lights or torches in honour of José Martí. This year (2015) was the 162nd anniversary of the birth of Jośe Martí, and it was celebrated to show that the fire of Martí is still alive among the generations. Most Cubans don't believe that the revolution started in 1959 with Fidel and Che, but that it began with Jośe Marti in 1895. I was one of many thousands who lined the streets of Habana and marched with burning torches in unusually cold weather. Also, in 2014, Cubans celebrated the 70th anniversary of the entry of the student Fidel Castro Ruz at the University of Habana.

Changes in Cuban and US Relations

On the morning of Wednesday 17th December 2014, I was attending lessons at Habana University when my mobile telephone vibrated with a text message. I ignored it and continued listening to the lesson. A few minutes later it vibrated again with another message that I continued to ignore. A call followed which I diverted to answerphone. After a few minutes I received more and more text messages so I switched off my phone as it was distracting others in the lesson.

Simultaneously, a loud exchange of dialogue could be heard from the corridor outside, which was not uncommon due to the architecture of the university, which amplifies normal conversations, but this was somehow different.

From outside the window I could hear cheering erupt from local houses nearby. What on earth is going on? I thought.

Well, Raúl Castro was addressing the nation on television, announcing that the final three members of the group known as the "five heroes" in Cuba had been freed from the US and had arrived back in Cuba that morning. For people outside of Cuba they would be better known as the Cuban Five - or Miami Five. The whole of Habana erupted (along with myself), taking to the streets in a huge celebration of their freedom.

Diplomatic relations were never going to be restored between Cuba and the US until the release of the Cuban Five. To know why, I recommend you read What Lies Across The Water by Stephen Kimber.

The presidential announcements by Barack Obama and Raúl Castro on 17th December 2014 concerning the restoration of full relations between Cuba and the United States could go down in history as an incredible victory of resistance against an imperialist power.

In what was a historic rapprochement after over 50 years of "frozen relations", Obama described the restored relations as "a new chapter among the nation of the Americas".

So, is it the case that now Cuba and Cubans have nothing to fear from the United States? Is everything hunky-dory?

Well, I have noticed that what people say and what they mean can be different, just as language used can change the way news is reported. For example, it is widely reported in pay negotiations that employers make "a pay offer" and the unions always make "pay demands". Employers are reported as being "reasonable" and the unions "unreasonable". The relationship between Cuba and the United States is no different.

On the same day as the presidential announcements on 17th December 2014, a new White House factsheet was issued - "Charting a New Course for Cuba" - that highlights that the United States has not changed its objectives, just its tactics & strategy.

Obama said: "We will end an outdated approach that for decades has failed to advance our interests and instead we will begin to normalise relations between our two countries." He stated regarding the blockade: "I do not believe we can continue doing the same thing for over five decades and expect a different result."

Obama has never, to my knowledge, said or acknowledged that the blockade was wrong, but that it was an "outdated approach" and "failed to advance our interests".

The concluding section of the new factsheet headed "Unwavering commitment to Democracy, Human Rights and Civil Society" states: "The US Congress funds democracy programming in Cuba...the administration will continue to implement US programs promoting positive change in Cuba." Is this positive change for Cuba, though? It would appear that the US remains committed to advancing its interest in Cuba.

A few days after the announcements, on Wednesday 24th December 2014, it was revealed that the US state department was making $11 million available for "regime change" programmes in Cuba.

Now, nobody calls them that – they're called "Bureau of Democracy, Human Rights and Labour". Grants of millions of dollars will be handed out to "US or foreign-based organisations" aimed at boosting "civil, political and labour rights" in Cuba. Priority is given that "emphasise the role of Cuban partners in developing and achieving pragmatic objectives". Now, these "objectives" are the same as before no matter how dressed up in the words of labour and civil rights they are.

Sound a little far-fetched? Well, read my chapter entitled, What Does USAID Really Do In Cuba?

The US Blockade of Cuba

To understand possible future relations between the Cuba and US, it's best to comprehend the difference between a blockade and an embargo, which was first explained to me by Cubans. A blockade is called this rather than an embargo because the latter could mean a legal, territorial action that prohibits commerce and trade with a specific country. Strikingly different, a blockade goes further and spreads extra-territorially, impacting on more than just commerce and trade.

A blockade cuts and closes any bonds in order to isolate the country from the outside world. This would include the effort to stop food, supplies and communications from entering or leaving the country.

It is designed to restrict economic, commercial, financial and other exchanges. The US blockade is estimated to have cost the Cuban economy more than 109 billion dollars.

The blockade under US law is called the Cuban Liberty and Democratic Solidarity Act (known also as the Helms–Burton Act) and it came into force in 1996. It helped to strengthen the blockade against Cuba, adding to the Torricelli Law, which was already in place.

The Helms-Burton Act doesn't just have a devastating effect on Cuba and Cubans, it has an impact on other countries and their citizens.

In 2014, French Bank BNP Paribas was fined $8.97 billion by the US for extending credits to Cuba and other countries. In 2012, British bank HSBC was also fined by the US. Other financial institutions have been investigated by US authorities including, Grench leaders Credit Agricole SA, Societe Generale SA, Germany's Deutsche Bank AG and Commerzbank AG, and Italy's largest lender, UniCredit Spa.

Travel companies based in Argentina and the Netherlands were fined $2.8 million and $5.9 million by the US for servicing travellers to Cuba. The manufacturer of Red Bull paid a fine of $90,000 to the US for filming a documentary on the island.

Cuba is denied life-saving medication and equipment. For instance, a number of antivirals are unavailable because the US holds a monopoly over their patents.

Health
Acquiring equipment and products in markets further away (from US), having to deal with agencies or intermediaries subsequently increases the costs as everybody takes their cut. In cases of child leukaemia in Cuba, where 75% were defined as "acute lymphoid", doctors were unable to provide the optimum treatment because it is US-manufactured. There are also obstacles in buying equipment which impact upon the diagnosis, control and prevention of congenital disorders and genetic diseases.

Food

Cuba is forced to spend more money to import food from further away, so freight costs are often 50% higher than if bought direct from the US. Living in Cuba I purchased toothpaste imported from Indonesia!

Education

Universities suffer losses of millions of dollars, causing academic programmes and projects to be cancelled, a loss of production and services and a lack of access to US technology, which means having to go further afield.

Finance

Cuba is prohibited from trading with US dollars worldwide, and this also prevents any financial institutions, such as the World Bank and the IMF (International Monetary Fund), from granting finance to Cuba.

Despite the consequences of the blockade, the free and universal healthcare in Cuba is ranked with the best in the world. Healthcare in Cuba is defined as a human right, unlike in other countries. This is also the case when it comes to education. Not only have the Cuban people benefited from achievements in education, but they have exported literacy programmes across Latin American. In 1961, the Literacy Campaign resulted in eradicating illiteracy in less than a year.

In 2003, Cuba helped to launch a programme called "yes, I can" in Venezuela. This eradicated illiteracy within one year by teaching more than one million people to read. Since 2003, the programme has progressed to "yes, I can continue", providing further education for more than one million students in Colombia, Bolivia, Nicaragua and Venezuela.

Yet Cubans witness and experience the impact of the US blockade of their country every day.

The return of the remaining "Cuban Five" was a small step in the right direction, according to my Cuban student friends at Habana University.

For more than half a century, the Cuban people have resisted the US blockade and other types of aggression and terrorism against them, at a monstrous cost. After outlining the agreements on the 17th December 2014, Raúl Castro said: "This in no way means that the heart of the matter has been solved. The economic, commercial and financial blockade, which causes enormous human and economic damage in our country, must cease."

One of my student friends said: "Cubans are like elephants, we never forget…the hard-right Cuban-American lobby has made a lot of noise since the initial announcements in December, but a presidential victory for Marco Rubio or Jeb Bush, who successfully campaigned against the imprisonment in the US of the convicted Cuban airliner bomber, Orlando Bosch, would result in not a step back, but a jump."

Members of the UJC (Young Communist League (Spanish: Unión de Jóvenes Comunistas) and FEU (University Students Federation Spanish: Federación Estudiantíl Universitaria) openly gave their support for what Mariela Castro, Cuban National Assembly member and gender rights campaigner, said in the press after the announcements. She stated: "If the US thinks these changes will bring Cuba back to capitalism and return it to being a servile country to hegemonic interests of the most powerful financial groups in the US, they must be dreaming…They are still dreaming and they are still planning."
This is a belief echoed by my Cuban friends, taxi drivers, general workers and doctors.

One Cuban woman I know told me: "We Cubans are one of the most educated populations in the world. Nothing changes until the end of the US Blockade, Cuba is removed from the terrorist list and Guantánamo Bay has been returned to us."

On 29th May 2015, Cuba was removed from the list of states sponsoring terrorism. This has eliminated another major obstacle towards restoring diplomatic ties.

Despite the changes, the US blockade of Cuba remains in place. So little has changed since December 2014. In July and August 2015, both countries have opened embassies and there has been an increase in the limit of money that can be sent by Cuban-Americans from the US, plus a reduction in restrictions on travel for Cuban-Americans to Cuba.

In order to rescind the laws of the US blockade, a vote in the US congress is required. The speaker of the house and the deputy speaker have reportedly said that there was "little appetite for a vote and they would not be tabling a vote as it was unpopular with republicans". It seems unlikely that there will be any major changes anytime soon, but more talking and no action. I believe that the recent dialogue between the two countries could be because since April 2014 there has been a steady stream of Russian and European countries sending diplomatic envoys to Cuba for talks about international development. The US therefore felt it could be missing out. The US was becoming increasingly isolated from the rest of the world in continuing the US blockade and the media profile of US contractor Alan Gross (imprisoned for clandestine acts in Cuba) had been increasing, thus acting as a thorn in the side of the US State Department.

Nobody claims that Cuba is perfect. I believe that the vast majority of Cuban people in Cuba do not want or need foreign interference in their country. I wonder if people in Iraq, Afghanistan, Libya and Egypt feel like they have experienced any more freedom or more democratisation than before the wars. In July 2015, Greece's debt crisis saw the opposite of freedom and democracy for the Greek people. The leaders of the European Union took the power of democracy from the Greek people and gave it to German, French, Belgian, Dutch and other European multinational corporations and banks (which the Greek government has no control over, either now or in the future).

The majority of Cubans feel that they have an active and important role in participating and shaping their country's future. They smile when they are informed that they have no freedom to do so by the US government, foreign press and commentators. There are a minority who would like to embrace capitalism but without losing the benefits of the revolution and socialism. A pink fluffy version of capitalism, where everybody is an entrepreneur and there is no destitution or starvation.

It should be up to Cubans what happens in Cuba. It is their country and we all still wait for the end of the US blockade.

What Does USAID Really Do In Cuba?

The United States Agency for International Development reported in the world press that it had secretly sent young people from Latin American countries to Cuba for the purpose of encouraging opposition and destroying the revolution. Also, an investigation conducted by AP (Associated Press) exposed the ZunZuneo project, which was based on using SMS message technology to promote destabilisation in Cuba.

Since 2009, young Peruvians, Costa Ricans and Venezuelans were sent to Cuba by USAID with the task of encouraging a rebellion on the island. The investigation revealed that "travellers worked undercover, often posing as tourists and travelled around the island scouting for people they could turn into political activists".

The group used cover approaches commonly employed by intelligence services, such as fronts and lies, secret lines of communications, encryption, promoting exchanges with overseas agents, seeking intelligence information on Cuban society, psychological preparation of emissaries in case of detection by Cuban State Security and the use of codes in communications.

Sound like a James Bond film? Maybe not. It's more Austin Powers as the journalists reported that the project was plagued with "incompetence and risks".

The operation even continued after the arrest and sentencing of US Contractor Alan Gross, who I will write about later.

A Costa Rican called Fernando Murillo was one of the young men who worked on the project. The AP report stated: "Their assignment was to recruit young Cubans to anti-government activism". This consisted of arranging programmes disguised as civic activities - in one case a workshop in HIV prevention. Murillo was told to check in every 48 hours and was provided with security codes. "I have a headache," for instance, would mean he thought that Cubans were watching him. USAID hired the firm Creative Associates International, which was also involved in the creation of the ZunZuneo programme.

It was revealed that the "operation often teetered on disaster...there was no safety net for inexperienced travellers, the work was explicitly illegal in Cuba".

From emails obtained by the investigation after Alan Gross was arrested, USAID told their operatives that they considered suspending their plans to travel to Cuba. However, in April 2010, the Costa Rican Murillo was sent to Habana. Murillo was contracted by Creative Associates International with the purpose "to turn Cuba's apathetic young people into effective political actors".

Murillo met a cultural group called Revolution, a group of artists devoted to electronic music and film based in Santa Clara. The idea was to hold seminars to recruit new "volunteers" as he needed a theme that would draw recruits and still be sanctioned by the Cuban state.

In November 2010, Murillo started a HIV workshop that 60 young people attended. This was supposed to offer participants straightforward sex education on prevention. But documents obtained by the investigation reveal that it was used as a recruiting ground.

When Murillo was contacted in San José, Costa Rica, he said that he could not speak about the details of his Cuba trips due to a signed nondisclosures agreement. He said that he was not trying to do anything more than teach. "I never said to a Cuban that they had to do something against the government," he said.

In a six-page report sent from Murillo to Creative Associates International it was emphasised that workshops were "the perfect excuse for the treatment of the underlying theme". Further into the report Murillo revealed another objective, "to generate a network of volunteers for social transformation".

The founder of the artistic group Revolution, Manuel Barbosa, said in an interview in Santa Clara that the Costa Ricans never told him that they were working for USAID.

On 3 September 2010, Irving Perez, a manager at Creative Associates International offices in San Jóse called a Skype meeting and announced a change in strategy. He said: "Our programme will no longer rely on trips to Cuba, at least not as the backbone of the operation."

Instead of travelling to Cuba, they would try to help certain Cuban "star contacts" obtain visas to train in a third country.

Did the project fail, or was it unwanted attention? White House Press Secretary Josh Earnest declined to comment when questioned about the project. He said: "I cannot comment on the report published in the US Press as there are several inaccurate points. I invite you to go directly to USAID."

A USAID statement made by spokesperson Matt Herrick denied secrecy programmes in Cuba. "The United States Congress finances pro-democracy programmes in Cuba to increase Cubans access to more information and the strengthening of civil society. All programmes carried out in Cuba are available to the public via the internet foreignassistance.gov. This work is not a secret, it is not covert and it is not illegal."

Just as in the case of the Zun Zuneo programme, there are similarities in this new subversive programme under the category of unconventional war methods that have been used increasingly over the years. This form of warfare is best explained within the book Confessions of an Economic Hitman: The shocking story of how America really took over the world by John Perkins. This method seeks to achieve the aims of regime change and domination in countries the United States considers opposed to its interests, with no need of direct involvement of boots on the ground, with relatively lower costs for the aggressor, but the polar opposite for the victims.

Federal agencies receive millions of dollars from US tax payers for supposedly humanitarian work around the world, but this is being exposed, yet again, as being a front for intelligence operations.

Casa Particulars

Look for the white sign with blue anchor on the Casa.

ARRENDADOR DIVISA

Casa Particulars best described as bed & breakfast. Costing between $5CUC to £30CUC depending on when, where and length. Average prices are $10CUC to $15CUC.

Paladares, Restaurants & Cafeterias

Paladares are mostly small family-run restaurants. Restaurants are normally larger and mostly state-run or in the form of joint ventures. Cafeterias are a mix of both, sometimes the windows of people's homes.

Asturian Federation of Cuba

Habana Gourmet Restaurants
Habana Vieja

The Asturian Federation of Cuba is located one block away from the back of the Iberostar Parque Central Hotel and is a similar distance from the Hotel Plaza in Habana Vieja. The building was constructed in 1772 and is a brilliant example of Habana architecture. Today, the building houses three excellent restaurants, Habana Gourmet, La Xana and La Terrazzo. Set over three floors, the higher you dine the more you pay, so eat on the ground floor. There is a very cheap and local cafeteria on the ground floor on your right as you enter and there are bars upstairs. The restaurants offer Cuban fusion food, Italian and mixed grills of lamb, shrimp, octopus and fish. They cater well for vegetarians. My favourite is La Xana, the Italian on the ground floor because it is great food and cheaply priced, offering many pizza options and the choice of different sized bases, which is a rarity for Habana. The pasta is the best I've had in the city. I normally only eat pasta in two places in Habana and this is one of them. I eat there at least once a week.

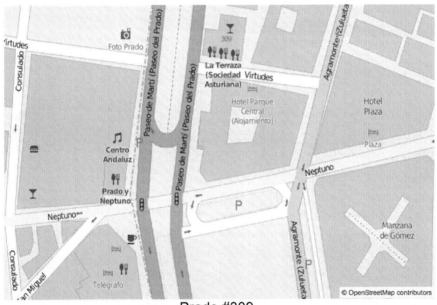

Prado #309,
In between Calle Virtudes y Animas
Habana Vieja
Tel: (+53) 7 864 1447
Email: info@havana-gourmet.com
http://www.havana-gourmet.com

Los Nardos

Located in the heart of Habana Vieja, opposite the Capitolio. It's easy to miss the entrance to this restaurant so look out for the queue! This is a famous restaurant in Habana for Cubans - a joint venture between the local Spanish Asturian Society and the Cuban state. The building houses two other restaurants so make sure you're in the correct one! You'll find it on the left at the top of the first set of stairs. Check the menu before sitting down. The food is excellent, offering an international menu and Cuban cuisine. Service is fast, efficient and charming. You'll find that it has the best prices for fish, interesting decoration and a cozy atmosphere. You will wonder how they got that grand piano up the stairs. Watch out for bottled water being placed on the table without being ordered. This is not a trick but style.

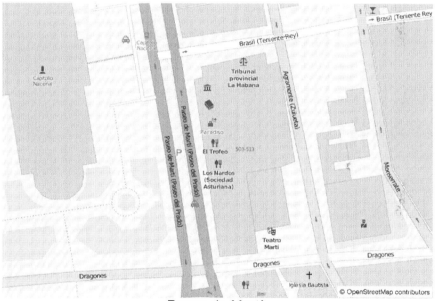

Paseo de Martí,
Between Brasil y Dragones
Habana Vieja

El Trofeo

This restaurant is located in the same building as Los Nardos. People dine at El Trofeo because they cannot get into Los Nardos. The food is good here too, but it can feel a little claustrophobic and does not have the same panache. Cheaper than Los Nardos, but bigger with its portions, the service is friendly and the rum is priced the same as the water. What's not to like?

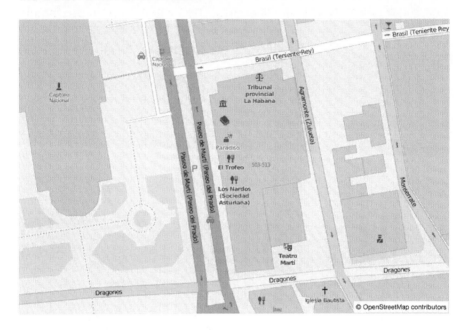

Paseo de Martí,
Between Brasil y Dragones
Habana Vieja

El Chanchullero de Tapas

Paladar and Bar

On Brasil street in Old Habana, the walls are covered with graffiti and photos, so it's very unpretentious. I have been eating here most months since 2014. From the street it may look intimidating, but go for it. On recent visits there have been queues, as this place has an amazing reputation for excellent cheap food. I can never keep up with its ever-changing menu, and my only disappointment is not being able to have what I had last time and that somebody has written over my writing on the walls!

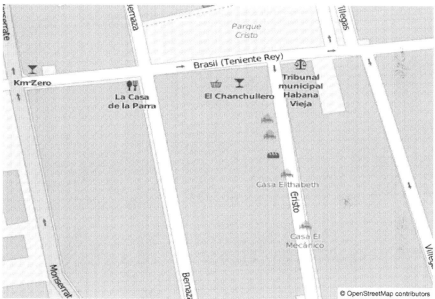

Brasil - Teniente Rey 457
Between Benrnaza and Cristo
Habana Vieja
+53 7 872 8227
+53 5 276 0938

The Italian Restaurant

Prado y Neptuno

Situated on the square of Parque Central, opposite the hotel Telégrafo, this restaurant has served consistently good food for the last 18 years. It is a spaghetti and pizza house, it is fast serving and the staff are pleasant. When entering look for the different coloured tablecloths as prices depend on where you sit. But don't worry too much, none of the food is expensive. If you want to watch football matches, others call it "soccer", then most European matches are televised in the bar.

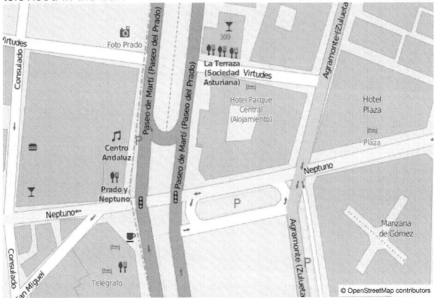

On the Paseo de marti Y Neptuno
Habana Vieja

Asociación Canaria de Cuba

Sociedad Canaria
Paladar

Here you'll get simple food, which is tasty and cheap. It's a must and you can even pay in national pesos. I visit this restaurant for lunch about once a week in Habana Vieja, and I live in Verdado!

The association members are descendants of Spanish people from the Canary Islands. It started as a charitable association in 1872 to provide healthcare, education and recreation for its members - more than 60,000 islanders emigrated to Cuba before the Cuban War of Independence in the early 19th Century. Hiding behind the Hotel Plaza within a red-brick building, it is opposite the Bacardi building. Just walk in and go up the stairs, or go through to the back hall and out into the courtyard.

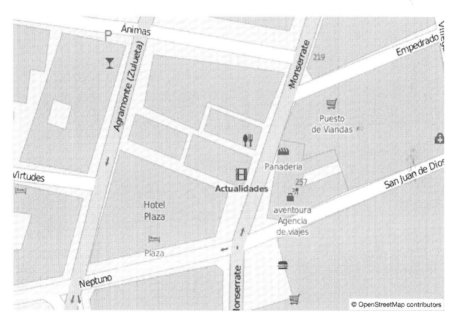

On Monserrate
Between Neptune y Animas
Habana Vieja

Café Paris

Years ago I loved this place as it looks really good, has a lovely interior and boasts a great band. But today the service is poor, the staff seem very unhappy and it is expensive when you compare it to other places. The food and drinks are good but maybe you are paying more than you need to.

It's situated on Obispo Street, which is the main street in Habana Vieja, which could be why the prices are so high.

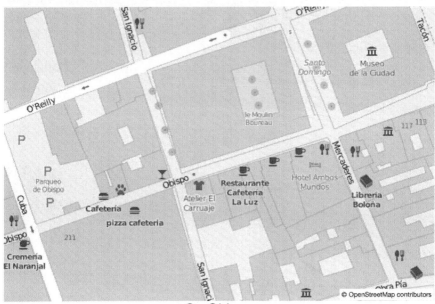

On Obispo
between San Ignacio y Cuba
Habana Vieja

Café Ambos Mundos

Restaurant

Located on the roof of the Ambos Mundos Hotel on Obispo Street, this restaurant will afford you some of the best views of Habana Vieja.

The hotel is famous for its one time long-term resident Ernest Hemingway. Ride the classic style open elevator to the top or, for a small charge, you can see Ernest Hemingway's Room 511, which is kept as a lovely museum. On the roof terrace there are impressive ceramic sculptures, non-invasive live music, excellent drinks and you can order a really wonderful lobster salad.

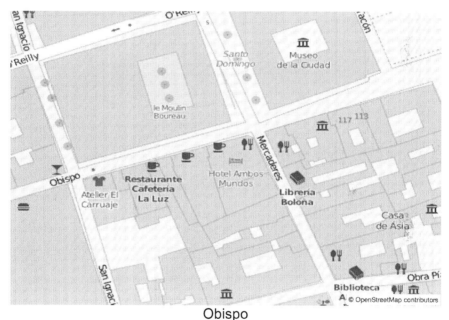

Obispo
Between Mercaderes and San Ignacio
Habana Vieja

La Dominica

Close to the Plaza de Armas, this is a very reasonably priced eaterie and makes a change from the offerings of some of the other restaurants – the portions are big too. I don't normally drink wine in Cuba, but here I ordered a Chilean red to accompany my shrimps in garlic olive oil. It was a perfectly fine dining experience in a very attractive setting. I sat inside but there is also al fresco dining.

O'Reilly
Mercaderes Y Tacòn
Habana Vieja
Tel: (537) 860 2918

Castropol Sociedad Asturian

Situated on the Malecòn, which has a brilliant balcony and arctic indoor air conditioning, Castropol is one of the best restaurants in Habana and Cuba. I have been dining here for years, seeing staff leave and then return again. Watch the sunset with a coffee and rum following an early dinner (the sun sets before 6.30pm for most of the year).

Downstairs is a pizzeria, but you want to eat upstairs in the restaurant, passing the bakery and cake shop on the way. The menu offers courses from the sea and the earth and all the food is better than excellent.

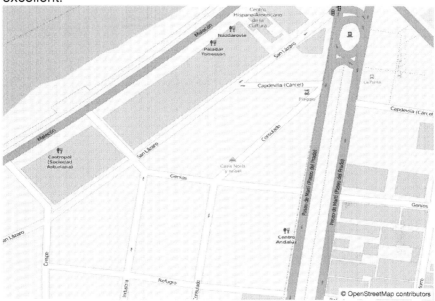

Malecòn
Between Genios and Crespo
Centro Habana

Nazdarovie

"We are Soviet women," the waitress informs me with a smile, "not Russian". Nazdarovie is a restaurant that was started by Soviet-Cuban women and it serves traditional dishes in wonderful Soviet themed surroundings. I wasn't sure if I was intimidated by her smiling reply or in love! Go for the beef stroganoff as it's excellent and served with mashed potatoes. The decor is very interesting and you have the option of either eating in a large air-conditioned room with big glass windows, or on a balcony with fantastic views of the Malecòn. The staff will tell you the history of the emigrating Soviet women and men who married Cubans and started families. I found them the most welcoming staff in Habana - or maybe they just liked me! The service is excellent and you'll be able to order food and drinks which aren't available anywhere else in Habana.

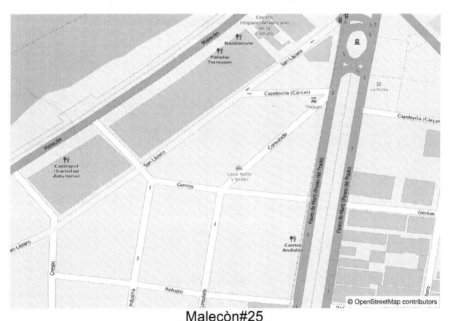

Malecòn#25
2rd or 3th floor
Between Prado y Carcel,
Centro Habana
Tel + (537) 8602947
http://nazdarovie-havana.com
info@nazdarovie-havana.com
comments@nazdarovie-havana.com

Casa del Taco

Paladar

You'll find Casa del Taco on the corner of Neptuno and Basarrata in central Habana, just down the road from the steps of the university. This is a real Cuban paladar, which you'll either love or hate – I love it. If you are, or were, a foreign language student at Habana University you will have eaten and had drinks here. Head upstairs for great food at amazing prices. You can choose from a huge variety of tacos, starting from $0.85CUC. The service is excellent and it's a great place to have a cheap lunch after class, hang out with friends over drinks or people watch from the terrace.

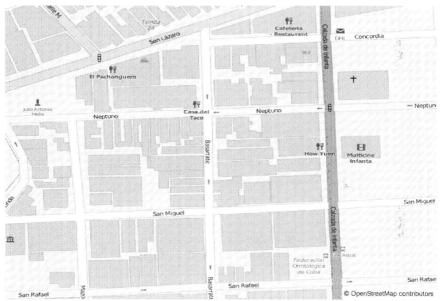

On Neptuno, Between Basarrata y MazònCentro, Habana

Fonda Paladar La Paila

La Paila is located just behind the Habana Libre Hotel in Vedado. An outdoor undercover paladar, it serves traditional Cuban food at affordable prices (if not as cheap as other places I've reviewed). The restaurant serves some of the best octopus in the city and its leg of lamb is the size of a small pony. When I visited we enjoyed our meals with a bucket of Cristal beers. Other options include rabbit with tasty side dishes and fresh juices.

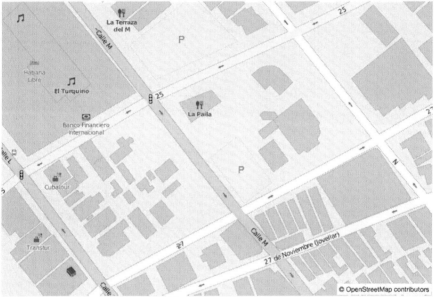

Calle M, between 25 y 27, Vedado

El Toke

Located right next to Las Vegas on Infanta, the prices here are higher than average but not too expensive. It's one of the few places in the city that knows how to make a chicken and shrimp salad properly. And while it's a typical Cuban hang out, it isn't off the radar of the average traveller. Open 24 hours a day, it has friendly and charming staff, fantastic drinks and a small outside seating area - but watch out for the Infanta traffic, it is so loud that you'll have trouble hearing your dining companions. Around the corner is a window into the kitchen that serves as a cafeteria. It offers the same food at cheaper prices and you pay in National Pesos. For a while I lived only a block away and would pick up a hamburger on my way home from a night dancing on the tiles!

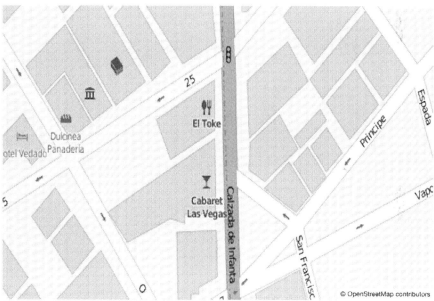

On Infanta, Between 25 y 27 Vedado

Duicinea Panadria

Want to sit and watch local Cuban life go by? Then take coffee and cake at Duicinea Panadria, which is situated around the corner from the Hotel Vedado. This small eaterie is at the heart of everyday life for Cubans. It's cheap, the cakes are delicious and it also offers sandwiches and pizzas. Go take a seat and listen.

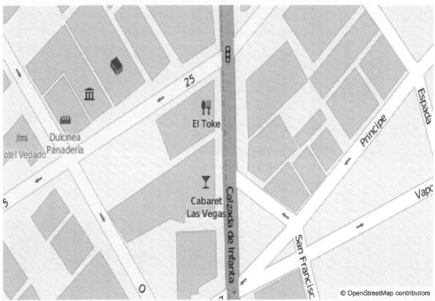

Calle 25, Between Calle 0 y Infanta, Vedado

Siete Mares – AKA Sad Fish Place

This has been nicknamed the Sad Fish Place by my friends as its outer walls are decorated with a marine theme of unhappy looking fish. And on my last visit the staff looked just as miserable. Ensure you ask for the menu in National Pesos. The food is fine for what you pay - less than $8CUC for 4 people – but don't expect too much. I've had many happy times here in the past, but have also been known to wait 2 hours for my food to arrive and have experienced maybe the worst service in the world. Maybe I just "wronged" the staff in a previous life. You will have a better experience I'm sure. Maybe!

On Calle, 23 between Calle J y I, Vedado

Don Quijote

This is situated next door to the Sad Fish Place (Siete Mares), but it's a much happier restaurant.

On New Year's Eve 2014, a group of us ate here, and I experienced the best pork I've ever tasted. I simply never knew it could taste like that! It's smaller than it used to be after the upstairs dining area and bar closed down, but it's still a busy place and serves a limited menu of Cuban cuisine.

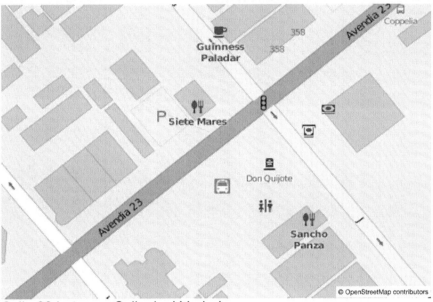

Calle 23 between Calle J y I Vedado

Guinness Paladar

No, unfortunately they don't serve Guinness here, but they do at the Canadian Embassy (the only place in Cuba where you'll find it). The owner simply liked the name. This is an authentic local paladar and even boasts a few tables and chairs. That may not sound like a big deal but it shows there has been an increase in the number of visitors to Cuba. Why? Well, only the best local paladars used by Cubans have tables, and even less have chairs. This restaurant serves pizzas, spaghetti and sandwiches. I eat breakfast here before uni on most days of the week and recommend the malt milkshake.

On Calle J between Calle 23 y Calle 21,Vedado

Los Primos

Paladar

In the middle of Vedado, just off Calle 23 and a hop, skip and a jump from Habana University, is Los Primos.

Open 24 hours a day and located on Calle H between Calle 21 and Calle 23, this is another example of a truly local Cuban paladar. Rachel will be on hand to serve you with my recommendations of either the chicken or the fillet of fish, which both come with rice, beans and salad. I started coming here in 2014 with my friend Saskia a few times a week, now I go almost every other day. The chicken (one of Saskia's favourites) is breaded and very tasty. Now my choice would be the fillet of fish. This is bigger than the plate and is cooked with lemon, garlic, onions and spices. Set in comfortable surroundings, it also houses a bakery which serves a wide range of bread.

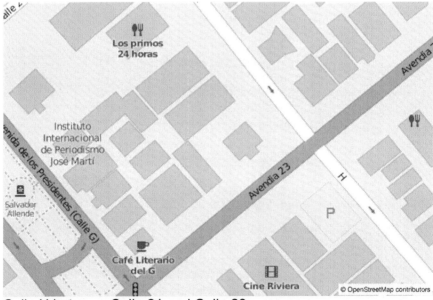

Calle H between Calle 21 and Calle 23.

Café Presidente

The food is mostly Italian, pizza, pasta and hamburgers all very good. El Presidente looks like a fancy expensive venue due to its very modern furnishings but it is cheaper than it looks. The desserts and drinks are impressive served with care & attentiveness.

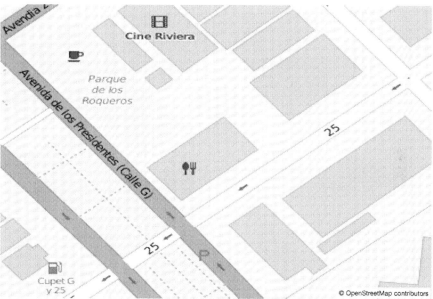

On the corner Avenida de los Presidents Y 25

Paladar La Moraleja

I ate in La Moraleja in the first month of it's opening and have been going back ever since, now it is expensive! It is set in an old home in Vedado, a few blocks away from the Habana Libre hotel, with themed decoration and air conditioning. Do look around at your surroundings, you will find the time. All the waitresses are extremely hospitable and will be very attentive to your table, just hold on to your husbands! All the food here is excellent, so I recommend all the dishes, lobster, chicken cooked in a stew pot, juicy shredded beef, try the rice with almonds and the Paladar is well know for its lamb, but leave room for the desserts!

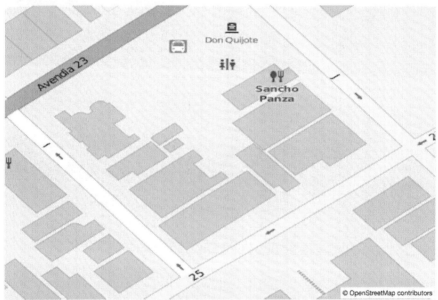

On Calle 25 between J y I Vedado

Calle J

One street, littered with Paladares & Cafeterias

For a truly Cuban local experience, head to Calle J in Vedado near to the University. Calle J has over 30 places to try, remember you need national pesos. Most of the business comes from students and workers from the hospital nearby. Head over just before lunch to escape the crowds.

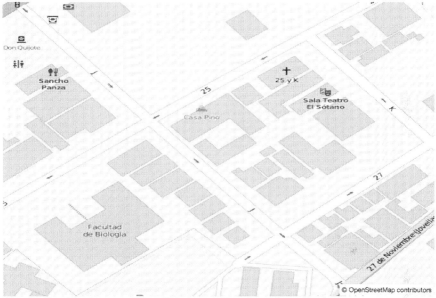

On Calle J between 25 y 27 de noviembre (joveliar)

La Catedral

Currently my favourite restaurant in Habana and also the rest of the city too! It is very popular for good reasons! First the drinks, Cuba Libres and mojitos are $0.95CUC and the strongest you will find throughout the island! The menu is in both Spanish and English. The food is brilliant and many options to try, plus the prices are medium to low. I would recommend this place to everybody including those on a budget. You are unlikely to find better in Habana in 2015 !

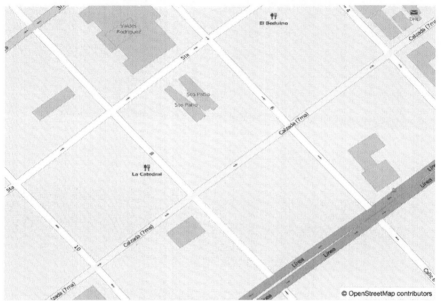

On Calle 8 between Clazada y 5ta in Vedado.

El Cocinero

El Cocinero is next door to Fábrica de Arte Cubano in Vedado. A rooftop bar with a decent selection of tapas designed platters, 6 of us ordered the entire menu and with drinks (we don't hold back) the total bill was $120CUC. Set in the tower of a former factory, you enter through a small door and up narrow stairs to the roof, don't worry it is very worth the trip. Reservations extremely recommended. Tel : 53 7832 2355

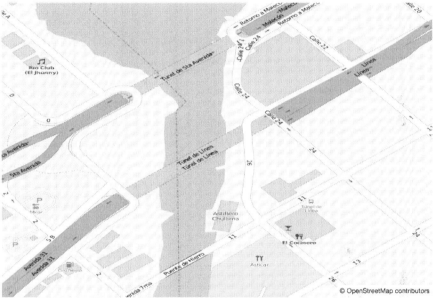

Calle 26 between 11 y 13 Vedado

Restaurante Paladar Café Laurent

A French styled restaurant in the middle of Vedado, Habana. Walking distance from the Habana Libre Hotel and located on top of a block of flats. Delightful evenings were spent here where I have enjoyed good food and a wide selective of wines at reasonable prices. The menu should appeal to both meat and fish eaters. Booking is essential for the outside balcony area and nobody will be disappointed dining at Café Laurent, test your French with the door staff before you enter the lift!

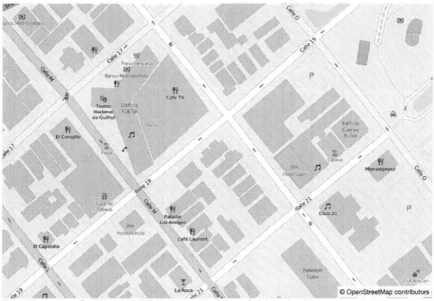

Penthouse, Calle M 257 between 19 y 21 Vedado
http://cafelaurent.ueuo.com

El Burrito Habanero

Mexican restaurant

El Burrito is a national peso restaurant with lots of character, big portions of great food and cheap prices! Ensure you try the juices and the mixed fried rice! If there is a queue, go around the corner to Los Primos or wait, it is worth it!

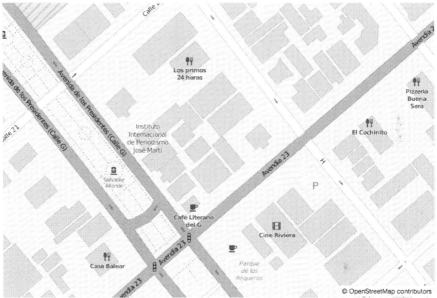

On Calle 23, between Avenida de los Presidents y H

Rio Mar

A paradise for fish lovers, there are tables inside or outside overlooking a small bay opposite Club-1830. This place is frequented by friends from various embassies around Miramar and for good reason too, the food is stupendous! Friendly staff, great views and the food, the food!

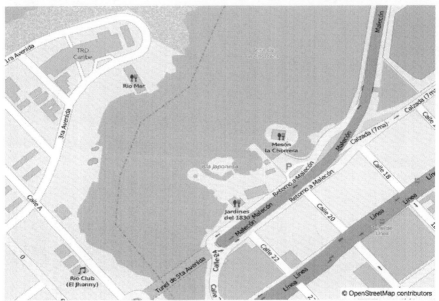

3ra y Final 11 La Puntilla Miramar

Habana Pizza

If you are looking for take away pizza, this is the true local place for pizza in National pesos, now it will not look like the pictures displayed but it tastes good and it is cheap!

Calle 23 – Between H & I

Riding The Guagua Around Habana

Every other day I use the local public bus services in Habana. In Cuba, the "buses" are called gauguas, pronounced "wawa" - like the sound a baby makes when it cries! As we are travellers and not tourists we do not need to use the Habana Tour Bus!

There are 17 main lines or routes, all with a P preceding the number from 1 to 16, and one P-C. There is a fleet of "MetroBus" buses covering Habana and surrounding areas with frequent gauguas about every 10 minutes in peak hours. In the past buses were commonly known as "camellos or camelitos" - that's Cuban Spanish for camels or little camels. This was because the buses had two humps. Most of these have now been replaced with modern Chinese manufactured buses called Yutong.

It costs everybody $1 National Peso (CUP) to go anywhere. Normally, due to the size of our groups, and with new travellers tagging along, using Maquinas/Colectivos is not practical. Groups of us have travelled all over the city to places like the Hemingway Museum, Club-1830, El Morro over the bay, Fábrica de Arte Cubano, Coppelia, La Rampa and even all the way to the beach and Parque Lenin. This is a brilliant way to explore and experience Habana.

TOP TIP

Riding the Guagua after Club-1830

After dancing the night away head over to Calle Linea and catch the bus. Club-1830 closes around midnight and there is normally a bus at around 12.15.

See maps on the web for more details.

Colectivo, Maquina, Taxi and Camións – What's The Difference?

Colectivos are like taxis that operate all over the island in different forms, night and day. They are like a bus operating on specific routes around the town or city, such as Habana or Santiago de Cuba. They also travel from city to city, for instance, from Habana to Santa Clara. As they drive along a route defined by the driver they drop off and pick up people on the way. Colectivos are mainly cars but in Santiago de Cuba they are motorbikes.

How safe are they? School children - boys and girls from the age of 7 or 8 - will take Colectivos across Habana alone. In other words, children every day enter cars, sometimes with only the driver (normally a stranger) and they arrive at their destination safely. At night, or more likely in the early hours of the morning, my Cuban and foreign female friends will catch a Colectivo, again alone, and again sometimes with only the male driver, and they always arrive at their destination safely.

Down in Santiago de Cuba cars used in this way are not permitted to enter the city centre (or so it has been reported). Instead people use motorbikes to get from place to place, sitting behind the driver who carries an extra helmet for customers. Rides cost between 10 and 20 National Pesos.

Maquinas or Maquina is a Spanish Cuban colloquialism; it's a local name for a classic car that refers to US models built before 1959. The "old American cars", in other words. However, when locals say it within a sentence they are most likely to be referring to a Colectivo or getting a taxi. Colectivos are normally a Maquina and/or a Russian made Lada. Sometimes to an untrained eye it can be difficult to distinguish the difference between a private Maquina, Lada and a Colectivo. Most will have a yellow or green "taxi" sign in the front windscreen or on the roof. Don't get them confused with the black and yellow Lada Taxis - these are not Colectivos.

Camións are large trucks which drive from town to town or city to city.

City and Habana based Colectivos will not take you directly where you may want to get to, but they will get you very close.

To use Colectivos effectively it helps to have a good sense of direction and know some general geography of the city. Get to know pick up points and when to get out. Don't dress like a tourist and, depending on the circumstances, limit speaking in anything other than Spanish.

Pick Ups - Stand on the side of major roads, at cross roads or junctions. Ensure you are standing on the correct side of the road for the direction of travel. When traffic is passing raise your hand, point a finger in the air and then hold up the same number of fingers as the number in your group. If there is a T-junction a few blocks down the street point with your finger in the direction you are wishing to travel in after the junction. When the car stops, tell the driver the major road or location you're heading to. Depending on where you are picked up, the Colectivos are likely to have passengers already who may swap their seat to be nearer the door (if they are getting out before you).

Drop offs - Just tell the driver you want to be dropped off or ask them to stop.

Say "aqui", which is "here". Pointing also helps. Have your money ready for when the driver pulls over.

In Habana the price is $10 National Pesos per person until you go under a tunnel in either direction - for instance to Miramar or Playa del Este - then it's $20 National Pesos.

Cuban Literacy Campaign

Since 1961, no nation has been able to match Cuba's incredibly rapid improvement in literacy. More than 50 years on, illiteracy rates remain at critical levels in less developed nations around the world. Strangely, illiteracy is increasing in my home country, the United Kingdom – one of the richest nations on the planet!

Cuban poet Jose Martí said: "To be educated is the only way to be free."

José Martí's philosophy and Che Guevara's ideology both lead this "battle against ignorance". Even in the revolutionary war, the rebels still made time for literacy work, as both Marti and Guevara recognised the liberating effect of education in resolving the problems of an illiterate and poverty-stricken country.

In 1961, thousands of young people, some as young as 11 years old, were able to reduce Cuban's illiteracy rate to below 4% in one year: an astonishing achievement. Even more important and amazing is how this happened, and the social change that took place as a direct consequence of teaching people to read and write.

For one year, night and day, young people - peasants, teachers and coordinators - worked collaboratively on the Literacy Campaign. It is very significant to relay the emotion of this experience and the political harmony that made the programme so successful.

In 1959, around 500,000 children didn't go to school and only 28% of young people aged between 13 and 19 had the opportunity to attend secondary school. At the same time some 9,000 teachers were unemployed. In 1961, more than one million Cubans were illiterate. Children from the age of 11 years old volunteered to help them, with over 100,000 participating. These heroic young people were named the "Literacy Brigadistas". To ensure the task could be completed within one year, a further 280,000 volunteer literacy teachers were enlisted.

The mass mobilisation of volunteers had never before been used to tackle illiteracy. The individual Cuban people were making a political decision to resolve the illiteracy crisis for themselves.

The aims of the literacy programme were more than just to teach people how to read and write. The idea was to create a permanent collaborative common bond between people. Thousands of young Brigadistas travelled and lived in the valley and mountain homes of the people they taught, becoming members of the family.

Brigadista Verde Olivo said in 1961:

"You can be a militia member, a teacher, a women's activist, active in rural co-operatives, a student in a peasant school. On all battlefronts, teaching, learning or working, together you represent an image of Cuban women today."

In April 1961, the US backed an invasion of Cuba at the Bay of Pigs. The literacy programme was at an early stage in this area of Cuba. Some schools were destroyed and some of the Brigadistas were taken hostage, much to the embarrassment of Washington and the Kennedy administration. Regardless, Cuba continued with its plans to teach people how to read and write.

Brigadistas were routinely hunted and executed by counter revolutionaries, as they were against the education of the population. They did this as a warning to others not to take part in the programme. Knowledge is power remember.

Three weeks before his 18th birthday, Conrado Benitez was working on a pilot literacy programme in the mountains when he was seized and executed by counter revolutionaries. He was tortured and suffocated by the gradual tightening of a rope around his neck and later mutilated. After his death student volunteers were organised into a brigade named in his honour, but he was only one of many volunteers who were killed by bands of counter revolutionaries.

Despite shortages of resources, such as petrol and vehicles, every effort was made for parents of the brigadistas to visit them in the countryside. This enabled mums and dads to understand the importance of the literacy programme and the issues affecting the countryside, which also led to new relationships between communities.

During the programme, 62 brigadistas lost their young lives due to illness or accident, which shows how hard conditions in the countryside were.

In addition to the literacy programme, thousands of young peasant women were given the opportunity to attend various courses in Habana. These courses included sewing, numeracy and health and hygiene. While in the capital they were housed in some of the city's most luxurious hotels, including the Hotel Nacional.

Within the last 57 years, Cuba has embarked on numerous literacy programmes with other countries, continuing its philosophy and ideology of free education and culture.

In the 1980s, a call to action resulted in 29,000 Cubans volunteering to teach in Nicaragua when only 2,000 were needed. Nearly half of them were women. When two Cuban teachers were killed in the country by sponsored terrorists, some 100,000 other Cubans volunteered to take their place.

In 2003, the Cubans helped launch a new literacy programme called "Yes, I Can" in Venezuela that eradicated illiteracy within one year by teaching more than one million Venezuelans to read. Since then the programme has progressed to "Yes, I Can Continue" and provides further education for more than one million students in Colombia, Bolivia, Nicaragua and Venezuela.

I would highly recommend visiting the Literacy museum in Havana located Ciudad Escolar Libertad, Marianao. Telephone 53 72608054 The museums director is Luisa Campos. For more details, see www.ecured.cu/index.php/Ciudad_Escolar_Libertad.

Some books are too important to ignore, so it is also recommended to read Shirley Langer's Anita's Revolution. Shirley brings the Literacy campaign alive! More details http://anitasrevolution.com

Medical Tourism

Medical tourism has been around in Cuba for a long time. In 2006, more than 1,000 patients from over 85 countries, including Canada, the United States, Mexico, Spain and the UK were admitted to Cira García Central Clinic for treatment. The hospital specialises in providing clinical, surgical and dental services, plus rehabilitation.

The specialties are wide ranging and include gynaecology and obstetrics, orthopaedics and neurosurgery. I have suffered from rheumatoid arthritis for 5 years and have been treated in Cuba by a wonderful clinical team of 15. I do not receive this level of care back in the UK, which is one of the richest countries in the world.

Living in Cuba I have experienced real Cuban local hospitals and been assigned a family doctor, just like the locals are, not medical tourism! At my initial clinical appointment with my rheumatologist at hospital, I was X-rayed from head to toe. Blood samples were taken that received more than 20 different tests. I was then seen by a raft of different specialists, including a physiotherapist and a nutritionist. My physiotherapist introduced me to a local man living in my area and I was signed up to do a Tai Chi class three times a week. My nutritionist asked me to keep a food diary for two months and monitored my weight as if I was an A-list celebrity.

My rheumatologist told me that if I was ever in pain, which is likely to happen at times - we call them flare-ups - I was to return to see her or a member of the team. She agreed it was unlikely that they would be able to offer me any solutions as I had all the medicine I needed to cope with my condition. Despite this, she was very insistent that if I was in pain I must seek them out.

During the cold and wet January in 2015, I experienced such a flare-up and I returned to the hospital and sought out my rheumatologist and some of the members of the clinical team. My rheumatologist and three others listened to me intently and then simply hugged me for about four minutes, also telling me how much they cared about me and that they were unable to offer anything more than I had already done myself. We then all left the hospital and went for ice cream. Now that's what I call medicine!

For others - Medical Tourism, check-ups for men cost $240 for which you receive two consultations with specialists, laboratory tests, a prostate ultrasound, X-rays and electrocardiograms. Cosmetic surgery is available, with liposuction of the waist, abdomen and thighs costing around $2,300.

It's important to know that the funds generated in this way are used to provide free treatment for Cubans, so yes there is a profit but a profit for the Cuban people and not private health care providers or drug manufacturers. Other services include cornea transplants, treatment for glaucoma and cataract surgery.

To find out more:
Cira García
http://www.cirag.cu/en
Address: Calle 20 No. 4101 esq. a Av. 41, Miramar, Playa.
Tel: (53) (7) 204 2811
Fax: (53) (7) 204 1633
Telefax: (53) (7) 204 2640
Email: publicas@cirag.cu

ELAM - Latin American Medical School

ELAM was established following Hurricane Mitch in 1998, when over 30,000 people, mainly from Central America, lost their lives. Cuba responded by sending over 1000 doctors to the regions affected in order to provide immediate disaster relief. This developed into a radical project to create a sustainable public health programme around the world. Instead of responding with emergency support they provided free medical training to foreigners so that they would be ready to respond in emergency situations, and in the meantime be self-sufficient.

From this, the idea of ELAM was born. Another institution also developed in Santiago de Cuba, training French-speaking students from Haiti, Mali and Djibouti (also for free).

Originally the first intake hailed only from the areas affected by Hurricane Mitch - Honduras, Nicaragua and Guatemala - and then extended to the rest of the hemisphere and African countries too.

ELAM is located in a former naval academy west of Habana. Its most basic objective is to train people from poor backgrounds (and in regions most affected by natural disasters) so that they are able to treat their fellow citizens.

At the end of 1999, there were 1,929 students from 18 countries studying at ELAM. The majority of them were from poor backgrounds and several were victims of torture or were the "disappeared" from Latin America. They were of different religions and had diverse political ideologies; some came from indigenous groups.

They were expected to study hard and return to their own communities or become part of other projects and programmes. They paid nothing for the tuition, food, accommodation or books, which is still the case today.

This may be the largest and most diverse medical school in the world, with no charge for any of the 20,000 students attending.

The philosophy of ELAM rejects the concept of privatisation of both buildings and health accessibility. It is based on providing central control of medical services and the distribution of it to all people. An essential principle within its training model is to empower local people to take on community responsibilities.

The Chernobyl Case

Even during the Special Period, when Cuba was faced with horrendous situations and challenges, it continued its policy of giving aid internationally to those considered in even greater need.

In 1986, a reactor at a Ukrainian nuclear power plant exploded. Some 150,000 inhabitants in a 30 km radius were evacuated, and 125,000 people died as result of the toxic fallout. Today in the region the thyroid cancer rate is 100 times the norm.

In March 1990, 139 severely ill Eastern European children arrived in Cuba to be cared for. Since then 23,000 people have been treated - 80% of them children. Again, this care was provided free of charge.

Each year around 700 to 800 children from the affected areas surrounding Chernobyl visit Tarara near to the east of Habana for medical treatment, and to recuperate. They stay for an average of between two and three months. It's estimated this has cost Cuba $300 million since the programme was implemented.

The first-generation victims were suffering from leukaemia and other forms of cancer that were caused by the immediate effect of the nuclear accident. Now the people arriving in Tarara have long-term medical conditions from the effects of radioactive exposure. These include genetic malformations and skin disorders, which respond well to the Cuban climate and medical treatment.

It shows the generosity of the Cuban spirit when you consider that around this time some Cubans felt betrayed by their former Soviet allies: before the collapse of the USSR, Ukraine had been one of its leading trading partners. By the 1990s the Cuban economy was in major decline and there were food scarcities and shortages of everything from spare parts to school supplies. Yet the revolutionary government's refrain maintained that: "children are born to be happy" regardless of where they come from, and despite the policies of their leaders. We all need to keep the world aware of the many selfless acts of Cuba. This small island republic, situated just 90 miles off the US coast, displays humanitarianism at its best.

Habana - Things To Do

There are many things to do and see in Habana. The city's five hundred year existence boasts the most diverse styles of architecture in the world (Baroque, Colonial, Moorish, Arabic, Eclectic, Art Deco and Art Nouveau). Choose from historical sights and landmarks, museums, theatres and concerts, parks and nature, bars, street food, cafeterias, restaurants and beaches.

Habana Vieja - Old Habana

You should start in Parque Central in old Habana, which is known locally as "Habana Vieja". Habana Vieja is best explored on foot, therefore a pair of comfortable shoes is essential. Watch out for the high heels of the locals! Some museums are closed on Mondays so go to the beaches at Playas Del Este, which are less crowded than at the weekend.

Calle Obispo

Obispo in Spanish means Bishop so walk down "Bishop Street" passing the famous El Floridita bar (on the corner of Obispo and Monserrate). It opened in 1817 under a different name "La Piña de Plata". El Floridita was made famous by US writer Ernest Hemingway and the El Floridita Daiquiri, a cocktail made with rum, lime juice and sugar. Keep walking or pop your head inside - today the El Floridita is one of Obispo's tourists traps!

On your left, walking with Parque Central behind you, you should see the InfoTur tourist information office. If you don't happen to have a map pop in and pick up a free one.

At the bottom of Obispo is Plaza de Armas, a square lined with palm trees that has a secondhand book market most days. In the middle of the square is a marble statue of Carlos Manuel de Céspedes who hailed from near Bayamo in the east of Cuba. He was one of the first to free his slaves in 1868 and declare Cuban independence, which was the beginning of the Ten Years' War of independence from Spain.

Located on the eastern side of the Plaza de Armas is Palacio De Los Capitanes Generales, which houses Habana's Museum of the City or Museo de la Ciudad. The building was the official residence of the governors of Cuba and the rooms have been restored and preserved with original colonial decoration that house exhibitions of art and historical artefacts. Before entering take a look at the street directly outside and you'll see that it is made of wood. One of the past governors didn't like to be woken up by the sound of horse and carriages on the cobbles outside in the early hours, so wooden ballast was used instead. Also, look at what has been used as barriers at either end of the street.

At the bottom of the plaza, located towards the Malecón, is a building steeped in history called the PA building. The construction dates from 1827 and was designed by Colonel Antoni de la Torre. I have been told by experts that this was the first building of Neoclassical architecture and has influenced Cuba ever since. Enclosed in the grounds is a bust of Christopher Columbus. In front of the building is a Ceiba tree and around the 16th November every year you will see hundreds of local "habaneros" walking around it three times and then tossing a coin into the roots before silently making a wish.

Just bordering the Plaza de Armas is a fort on the western side of the harbour of Habana. This is the Castillo de la Real Fuerza or Castle of the Royal Force.

Plaza de Vieja

If you're looking for more spectacular architecture then head to Plaza de Vieja. The plaza was declared a World Heritage Site by Unesco in the 1980s. Some of the funding for restoration projects comes from the profits from local hotels and restaurants. During the building restoration, residents were temporarily relocated with a legal guarantee that they would return to their home on completion.

In the Plaza you'll find the Planetario de la Habana, a scientific and cultural centre covering several floors with a reconstruction of the solar system and an astronomy observatory. The construction involved many institutes from around the world, including the Japanese government. You will be shocked with what is inside as the outside fascia has been restored and preserved, so you'll find yourself stepping from 1814 through doors into the future.

For those wanting a bird's eye view of Habana, take your camera and head to the corner of the plaza and the Camara Oscura on the top floor of the eclectic Gómez Vila building near the streets Mercaderes and Brasil. It is well worth the five flights of stairs to the top, or just take the lift. The Oscura Camera was a gift from the council of Cadiz in Spain.

watch prices

Santo Angel Restaurant, within the Plaza near to San Ignacio and Brasil, is the perfect spot to enjoy a meal, listen to music and watch the world spin by. The food is good and the experience very positive. Of course, I would advise reviewing the prices before ordering as it is a little expensive. An alternative is Cafe El Escorial, located diagonally across the Plaza from Santo Angel, near streets Inquisidor and Muralla. This is one of the better places to go to eat and have coffee. It is a great spot to sit and people watch, read a book or listen to music.

good review

114

In the last corner of the plaza we have La Factoria Plaza Vieja, Habana's first microbrewery (its sister company is located on the docks). Serving three types of cold beer: light, dark and medium, patrons sit on sturdy, well crafted wooden benches either inside or out on the Plaza.

Beer can be drunk from tall cylinders with a tap at the bottom and the atmosphere is great - just don't eat the food, it's ridiculously overpriced and the portions are small. To eat, head to the sister company near the docks - Almacén de Madera y Tabaco

Almacén de Madera y Tabaco

Habana's Second Microbrewery - Bar and Restaurant

Located opposite the Arts and Crafts market on the docks of Habana, this is a fantastic example of investment within Cuba. Sit on the patio and watch the sunset on the waterfront bay area. Behind is a great view of Iglesia de San Francisco de Paula Church. It is here that I learnt the names of the different types of beer served: Marzen, Blonde, and Dunkel. I have spent "some time" with German friends sampling the different styles here, as well as in the company of the local microbrewery master who was eager to share his passion and knowledge on Cuban techniques. The master brewer was anxious to know if the Caribbean microbrew got the seal of approval from the taste buds of German beer drinkers. (He did not care for my opinion!) It passed well. I would encourage everybody, whether novice or expert, to visit this brewery and taste a true local beer. For non-beer lovers there is the view! The restaurant is large and service might be slow, so just sit back and relax or head over to the Arts and Crafts market.

Mercado Artesanal San José

Located opposite Almacén de Madera y Tabaco, Habana's second microbrewery bar and restaurant, you will find the Arts and Crafts market. If shopping is your thing then don't miss this wonderful indoor place - it is huge. Wander around to find paintings, sculptures and souvenirs. While exploring, look out for the creative recycling and reuse of all types of materials. One example would be the reuse of the ring pulls from local beer cans. The green Cristal pulls and the gold Bucanero pulls are crocheted into all sorts of purses, handbags and much more. There is also a cafeteria and money changing house on site.

El Museo del Ron Habana Club - The Rum Museum

This is good fun if you like rum and offers an informative and interesting insight into the process of rum making, which is well linked to the history of Cuba! Check the timings for tours in various languages: English, French and Russian. The museum is located on Avenida del Puerto, better know as the Malecón, only two blocks from the Plaza de Vieja. Past street Muralla heading down Mercaderes and then turn left into Sol street down to the Malecón.

Habana Cathedral

Located in the Plaza de la Catedra, the Cathedral of The Virgin Mary of the Immaculate Conception, is one of eleven Roman Catholic cathedrals in Cuba. Built by the Jesuits in the late 1700s, it is the best example of Baroque architecture in Cuba.

Within the Plaza de la Catedra is a life-sized statue of Spanish flamenco dancer Antonio Gades, which leans against a pillar in front of the Palacio de Lombillo. Antonio Gades brought this type of dance to world recognition and is revered by Fidel.

Directly opposite the Catedra is the Museo de Arte Colonial, which I visited as part of a Habana University class excursion with a group of fellow students. We were informed that the museum was once a famous house owned by Don Lus Chacon, a military governor of Cuba. The building has been completely restored and in many rooms you can see all kinds of colonial artefacts and furniture. Make sure you get a good look at the stained glass windows!

La Bodeguita del Medio

La Bodeguita is a restaurant and bar made famous by its past customers who include Salvador Allende, Nat King Cole and Gabriel Garcia Marquez. It opened in 1942 and its rooms are full of fascinating objects; framed photographs and signatures cover the walls throughout the building. It is bigger than you think; a bit like Doctor Who's Tardis. The eye-watering $5CUC mojitos in the bar downstairs are OK, but you are hopefully paying for the atmosphere.

El Morro - Castillo de los Tres Reyes Magos del Morro

The Fortress

Are you ready for adventure, to visit where pirates and buccaneers wished to wander? And do you want to get to "El Morro" like a local for $1 National Pesos (CUP)? You have two options then. Either take a ferry across the bay to Casablanca (see Museo del Che on the way) and walk from there, or catch the local P11 bus.
You can find the bus stop for the P11 opposite the Capitolio between Dragones y Máximo Gòmez and get off at the first stop after exiting the tunnel (your returning bus stop is just opposite this stop). Otherwise catch the ferry from the bottom of Calle Santa Clara on the Malecón opposite Iglesia Ortodoxa Rusa. The terminal looks like an abandoned building, ensure you queue on the left for Casablanca, look up for the signs.

I recommend visiting El Morro in the late afternoon, staying until 9pm for the cannon ceremony.

El Morro was started by the Spanish, but in 1762 the fortress was captured by the British before being returned under treaty terms around a year later. "Morro" means a rock which is visible from the sea, such as a navigational landmark or port entrance. It was originally built around 1589 as Habana had been experiencing raids by pirates. To protect Habana, at the entrance of the harbour every night at 9pm, a long chain was stretched out across the water from the other side of the bay to El Morro. This would stop ships entering the bay. Simultaneously, a cannon was fired to inform the sailors of nearby ships that the harbour was closed and they would need to drop anchor out at sea.

Every night of the year at El Morro the firing of the cannon is recreated in a ceremony with Cubans wearing British solder's uniforms from that era. More interesting is the response from the mainly Cuban audience – their reaction to the cannon fire is more thrilling than the show itself. Cubans love this event! It certainly gives you a feel of what pirates and the British must have experienced centuries ago. The location also has excellent views over Habana.

Plaza de la Revolución

Originally the plaza was called "Plaza Cívica" (Civic Square). The construction of this and the José Martí monument started during the time of Batista and was completed after he fled the country in 1959. In the same year it was renamed "Plaza de la Revolución (Revolution Square).

Since 1959, many rallies and celebrations have taken place in the square, including the September 2015 visit of Pope Francis who conducted his first sermon celebrating Mass there.

Other rallies and celebrations are common throughout the year. Some of the biggest take place each year on 1st May and 26th July. The former is International Workers' Day, which is also commonly known as Labour Day. This celebrates "workers" around the world and originates from a successful campaign for an eight-hour workday. 26th July is the date of the attack on the Moncada garrison in Santiago de Cuba in 1953 and was adopted as the name of a revolutionary movement.

On 22nd December 1961, hundreds of thousands of Cubans marched heroically to Plaza de la Revolution carrying giant pencils following the eradication of illiteracy in less than one year. They chanted "Fidel Fidel, tell us what else we can do". "Study, study, study!" came the reply.

A lift next to the José Marti monument takes you to the top of the 109m tower. On the other side of the plaza are the famous images of Camilo Cienfuegos and Che Guevara, with his well known slogan "Hasta la Victoria Siempre" (Until the Final Victory).

Bacardi Building

You will find the Bacardi building behind the Plaza Hotel on Monserrate, between San Juan De Dios and Empedrado. Go to the roof terrace of the Plaza Hotel opposite and wander about until you can see the Art Deco Bacardi building from an angle most never witness! This was the largest building in Habana at the time of its completion in 1930, and it was commissioned by the Bacardi Rum Company. Travellers can see the sights and landscape from the top roof balcony of the Barcardi building via a lift and a narrow and steep staircase. The sights of Habana are better than the building.

The Bacardi family has an interesting and controversial history. In 1861, a French born distiller transferred his expertise to two brothers who then went on to create the company "Jose Bacardi y Cia" in Santiago de Cuba. A few years later, one of the brothers bought out the other shareholders and eventually his sons Facundo and Emlio inherited the business and distillery.

It seems that for a long time the Bacardi family and business received protection from the US. In 1954, when one of the Bacardi children was kidnapped, a US consul arrived in a helicopter from Guantanamo Bay within hours, shortly followed by an FBI team flown in directly from Miami. Within 12 hours the kidnappers were dead and the child had been returned. In 1957, the Bacardi HQ was relocated and the trademark was registered in the Bahamas due to concerns surrounding the shaky ground of Batista's coup d'etat and the rise of revolutionary forces.

In 1960, most companies and businesses in Cuba were nationalised, including Bacardi. Most foreign businesses accepted the compensation offered, but Bacardi refused and since then the company has been linked with counter revolutionary action groups and CIA sponsorship operations. Bacardi is neither produced nor served in Cuba and the company supports the US blockade of Cuba.

Further information: Bacardi: The Hidden War by Hernando Calvo Ospina ISBN no: 0-7453-1873-8

Paseo del Prado

Paseo del Prado is a beautiful street or promenade on the dividing line between Habana Vieja and Central Habana. It runs the whole length of Paseo Marí, all the way to Capitolio. Today, most see the Prado starting at Neptuno Street and finishing at the Malecón (seawall).

The Prado was where people, couples and especially families would go to walk in order to be "seen" and therefore be part of society. Today it is not much different and it's where the locals go to sit and watch the world go by, play dominoes or chess and, for the children, skateboard. The Paseo is lined with trees and marble benches that were designed in 1772 by a French landscape architect. Either side of the Prado the buildings are styled in themes from Madrid, Paris and Vienna.

The best time to stroll along the Prado would be at the weekend when the promenade becomes an artists' market.

Museo de la Revolución - Museum of the Revolution

The museum is located in what was the Presidential Palace of Batista and it became a museum following the Revolution. It was designed by Cuban and Belgian architects who incorporated Neoclassical features and it was decorated by Tiffany and Co. Exhibits are devoted to the revolution and the Ten Years' War of Independence from Spain.

Situated outside is the Granma Memorial and other vehicles and tanks used in the revolution. Granma was the yacht used by the revolutionaries to sail from Mexico to Cuba in 1956. It's so securely enclosed that you can hardly see it until you are up close.

El Malecón

The Malecón is the Spanish word for seawall. Habana's Malecón stretches 5 miles (or 8km) from Habana Vieja across Central Habana, ending in Vedado. Today it is still popular with Habaneros, Cubans from other cites and towns, lovers and fishermen.

Along the Malecón there are some monuments you should look out for, including for people like, General Máximo Gomez, Antonio Maceo and Calixto García and the monument to the victims of the USS Maine.

For locals, the place to be at the weekend is at the junction of La Rampa (23rd Street) and Malecón, so it can get very busy. This part of the Malecón has many purposes; it's a general meeting place for friends and families and the place to find a boyfriend, girlfriend, husband or wife. While the rest of the world has online dating, Habaneros have the Malecón!

At the bottom of La Rampa, stopping at the petrol station on the corner, you'll find the LGBT community. To the right, in the direction of the Hotel National and the José Martí Anti Imperialist platform, groups of friends, families and those who are already within a relationship often congregate. To the left, starting at La Rampa in the direction of El Morro & Habana Vieja is the best place to find a romantic relationship for Habaneros, the further along the Malecòn, the longer the commitment. There are regular concerts at the Josê Martí Anti Imperialist Platform, which is in front of the US Embassy.

Heladeria Coppelia

Ice Cream, Ice Cream, Ice Cream!

Named by Celia Sánchez after her favourite ballet, this place is all about ice cream. The Coppelia in Habana is reported to be one of the largest ice cream parlours in the world.

A major city landmark, it is shaped like a flying saucer and covers a whole city block. It also features in the film Strawberry and Chocolate, which is one of the most widely viewed Cuban films ever.

Cubans love their ice cream. In the 1960s, a project was started that sent Cubans on a mission to find the best flavours. Covering Canada, Sweden and the Netherlands, the project was so scientific that it not only covered taste, but also the means of production en masse.

Museo Hemingway Finca Vigia

Located around nine miles east of Havana in the town of San Francisco de Paula is the home of writer Ernest Hemingway called Finca Vigia meaning the "lookout house".

Beautifully restored with original furnishings, his books and the desk where he wrote "for Whom the Bell Tolls and The Old Man and the Sea." As well as the 38 foot fishing boat called "Pilar", the lookout and swimming pool. It is an exquisite collection of the history of Hemingway. Just Go!

Carretera Central (Calzada de Guines) Between Stringer y Vigia - San Franciso de Paula
San Francisco de Paula | Carretera Central Km 12.5, Havana, Cuba
Phone Number: 53 7 891 0809

House of José Martí (Casa Natal De José Martí)

Leonor Pérez No 314 between Picota y Avenida de Bégica

The house where Jose Martí was born on 28th January 1853 is now a museum in the memory of the Cuban independence leader. The museum hosts artefacts, paintings, photographs, his desk and diary as well as a sequential informative outline of Martí's life and history of the 10 year war for Cuban independence. For Spanish speakers' the curator and guides are very happy to elaborate on plaques and artefacts, they are very proud of Martí.

Habana's Cemetery

The cemetery was founded around 1876 and is located in the neighbourhood of Vedado. The cemetery's full correct name is Cementerio de Cristóbal Colón named after Christopher Columbus. It covers about 140 acres and is well known for the quality and quantity of marble sculptures, mausoleums & family chapels. My guide, a gardener at the site informed me that this place is very important in terms of history and architecture.

Look out for an enormous monument dedicated to firefighters who lost their lives in the great fire of 17th May 1890. I also learnt that after three years remains are removed from their tombs, boxed and placed in chapels. Among the occupants are the parents of José Martí, Alberto Korda the photographer who captured the famous image of Ché, Federico Capdevila, a Lieutenant Colonel of the Spanish Army who defended the Cuban students of Medicine in 1871. Others include Celia Sánchez Manduley, Haydée Santamaría, members of the Buena Vista Social Club, Ibrahim Ferrer & Ruben Gonzalez, poets' Nicolás Gullén & Alejo Carpentier. Also the marble tomb of Catalina Lasa designed by René Lalique. (See Casa de la Amistad)

Miniature Habana (Maqueta de la Habana)

An incredibly accurate scaled model of Habana that provides a great grasp of the harbor, neighbourhoods and the old city layouts. If you're lucky you might eavesdrop on a guided tour and learn something new, hang around for the light change too.

Calle 28 | Between Avenidas 1 and 3, Miramar, Havana,

Our Lady of Kazan Orthodox Cathedral

In Spanish the Cathedral is called Catedral Ortodoxa Nuestra Señora de Kazán. A very impressive pure snow white five domed Russian Orthodox structure, built in ancient architectural tradition that started in 2004! Located on the waterfront opposite the port to Casablanca. On the corner of San Pedro and Santa Clara.

Open between 09:00 - 16:00
Services held daily at 10:00am and Vigil at 17:00

San Pedro Ave. and Santa Clara
http://ow.ly/RP8by

Café O'Reilly

Calle O'Reilly 203, at the corner of Calle San Ignacio

Try to avoid the "tourist" and experience a true essence of local culture, this Café has stayed pretty true to its roots, well as much as it can being located on the corner of Calle San Ignacio on O'Reilly in heart of Habana Vieja. Come for the aromatic and variations of coffee, also serving sandwiches, ham & cheese or cheese and ham, fresh juices and milkshakes ! A good oasis to sit and refresh either upstairs or downstairs after walking in the sun!

Fusterlandia

José Rodriguez Fuster - Picasso of the Caribbean
http://ow.ly/ROWFk

You have to see it to believe it. This fabulous celebration of creativity - STUNNING!, without visiting nobody will understand what it feels like to wander around a land of art ! You need imagination and to love colour to really appreciate.

Fusterlandia is ceramics, engravings, paintings and drawings by José Rodriguez Fuster in the town of Jamanitas located on the outskirts of Habana. Over 10 years work of rebuilding and decorating over 80 houses in the artist's neighbourhood. The art now is protected and cherished as Cuban culture. Come and check out the chess park with giant boards and tables as well as the ornate murals and domes. Josê's son Alex should be on hand to act as translator but Alex also is a talented artist himself. 5ta Avendia y 226, Jamanitas.

University of Havana

88 Steps to the Alma Mater sculpture located just in front of the magnificent campus. Come and see brilliant architecture that's not only impressive to see but also steeped in history. You are free to wander about in the week, but it is closed at the weekend. UH (University of Habana) is made up of many faculties and research centres such as the natural sciences, mathematics and computer science, social sciences, humanities, economic sciences and where

you may find me attending the faculty of Spanish for foreigners. This was the University attended by Fidel Castro in the 1940s and become a centre of anti Batista protests so Batista closed the University in 1956! Today education is free for all and defined as a human right in Cuba.

Where best to learn Salsa

Casa del Tango

Calle Neptuno 309, corner of Neptuno and Galiano. They teach tango and salsa they are very professional and it costs between $5 - $10CUC per hour depending on the total number of hours. Don't fall in love or date your teacher!

La Casa del Son

This dance school has an international reputation within the dancing community covering most of Europe and beyond.

This is more expensive than Casa del Tango, maybe due to the venue and teaching but both schools are good. Here too you can find private lessons for a good price between $10 - $15CUC per hour and the teachers have more patience than others. The school hosts social nights and shows. Great laid back people like normal. Go as a beginner or pro and ensure you try to learn rueda before you leave!

Empedrado # 411 e/ Compostela y Aguacate. La Habana Vieja. La Habana. Cuba
(+537) 861 6179
(+53) 5 264 1047
lacasadelson@bailarencuba.com
http://ow.ly/ROWKV

Dancing Holidays

With over 18 years of organising groups from 30 to 300 people Eagle Activity Tours is maybe one of the best to book for a full dancing holiday in Cuba. All levels of dancer are catered for ranging from beginner to advanced. I have met groups over the last few years who have had a spectacular time! Check out www.salsatours.co.uk

Edificio Focsa

The FOCSA Building located in Vedado is the tallest building in the whole of Cuba not just Habana! The building was started in 1956 and completed over 2 years later. There are two restaurants, the first on the ground floor "El Emperor" and "La Torre" located on the 33th floor with a striking 360 degree view of Habana ! There are also cafeterias, shops, a theatre, commercial offices and radio and television studios.

Calle 17, 19, M and N in Vedado

Estadio Latino Americano

The Estadio Latinoamericano is the home of Havana's baseball team the Industriales! Located near to the Plaza de la Revolución. Cubans' love baseball! Fans are enthusiastic and animated. The noise in the stadium can rival a concert! Baseball games were free with funding from the state but Cuban's voted to contribute individually! Check with your Casa owners about times of games! Calle Avenida 20 de mayo y Pedro Perez

La Cabana de Che Guevara

Che's home in Habana is located over the bay near to Casablanca and definitely has fabulous views across the city. Very informative about Che's life, with lots of photography and his personally belongings and items used during his life like his camera, coat and radio. Incredible views from the balcony, afternoons are best for photos when the sun is behind the casa.

Museum of Decorative Arts

If you enjoy art, architecture and history this is the place for you! Located in Vedado Calle 17 y E. The mansion was built in French Renaissance neo-classical style. Provides it a good indication of the differences between the rich and poor in Habana before the Revolution. The museum is packed with decorative furniture and art collections from UK, France, Italy, Japan, China and a small collection of Tiffany and art deco glassware.

Casa de la Amistad

Casa de la Amistad is the House of Friendship used by **ICAP,** (*the Cuban Institute for Friendship with the Peoples. In Spanish: Instituto Cubano de Amistad con los Pueblos*) **CTC** (*The Workers' Central Union of Cuba. In Spanish: Confederación de Trabajadores de Cuba)* and international solidarity groups. The mansion was built by a very wealthy Cuban sugarcane plantation owner Juan Pedro Baro to equal the beauty of his beloved Catalina Laza. This love story was a big scandal at the time as Catalina was already married at the time and as there was no divorce in Cuba. When the couple attended a public performance in a Habana theatre, the rest of the audience left as a public display of disapproval and humiliation. The mansion was built with the finest marble from Italy and famous French Lalique glass was used for light fittings and for the windows in a eclectic style with Florentine renaissance facades and the interiors are art deco with Egyptian references.

At the front of the building there are two large terracotta columns either side of the entrance with Doric capitals and two very large windows with Florentine designed metal work.

You enter a large hall with a marble floor decorated with pyramids with black squares and rectangles leading to a magnificent marble staircase. Behind the mahogany doors is a library and dining rooms.

There is an onsite restaurant and most Saturday nights events are arranged where you are entertained by singers, dancers and drummers ending with an audience salsa of course!

Paseo No 416 Between Calles 17 & 19, Vedado

Casa de Las Americas

Casa de Las Americas is housed in a stunning art deco building. It was founded by Haydée Santamaría, who was one of the first members of the 26th of July Movement. The venue is a Cuban contemporary culture legacy with central aims to promote socio cultural connections and communications between Cuba, the Latin Americas and the rest of the world. It is the home of an literary press of the same name. There is bound to be a worthwhile poetry reading, performance or a conference that will interest you. Just swing by and check out what's posted in the lobby or check out the web site. http://ow.ly/ROWOL 3ra y G, Vedado

Teatro Nacional de Cuba

There are two main theatre stages here, the Avellaneda, Covarrubis Halls and a theatre workshop space. In the bigger Avellaneda the stage and orchestra pit are spacious. Seating is basic with very good views of the stage and not obstructed by the people in front. I have seen ballets, plays of Shakespeare and classic music recitals. An absolute delight, my friends were taken by surprise on how wonderful these performances were! These events are definitely a must see. http://ow.ly/ROWQb

Paseo y 39, Plaza de la Revolciòn, Tele 785590 / 704655 email tnc@cubrate.cult.cu

"A fool and his money are easily parted."

Notice it is always written as "his money" and not "her money". This is because most women are not that stupid!

Well, most men only go to the doctor or dentist when told to do so by their mother, wife, daughter or girlfriend. As for integrity, it's really easy: don't cheat, don't lie and if you happen to procreate and don't want to have a relationship with the mother of your child, you still have an obligation to be a father, regardless of how hard this might be.

Now, I don't intend to stereotype, but this leads me to the story of two men I met recently, both of whom are in their early 30s. I explained at different times to the two of them (they never met each other) about the possible types of relationship for foreigners with Cubans. However, this information went in one ear and out the other. The first guy, who I met in 2014, had two mobile phones and a camera stolen from his apartment after returning with somebody he had just met on a drunken night out. I met the other chap the following year and can only describe him as an idiot. This is because he had money, a camera, phones and soap stolen on more than one occasion.

So what did I explain both times while sitting opposite them in Club-1830 and a bar called Torreón de la Chorreraon?

True Love does happen and people do marry, have children, grandchildren and live the rest of their lives together, either living in Cuba or somewhere else. I know couples happily living in Habana, Santa Clara and in other parts of the world, including a Dutch man who emigrated to Santiago de Cuba after marrying a local woman in the early 1990s.

If you are going to enter into a relationship anywhere in the world be realistic as your expectations may differ to your partner's. Take time for the relationship to develop and maybe don't rush into marriage.

Over recent years the phenomena of the "holiday romance", or, in Cuba, the holiday boyfriend or girlfriend has developed to avoid the attention of the authorities. It may be a form of prostitution but it's unlikely that any actual cash is exchanged. Instead costs relating to hotels, restaurants, gifts, shoes, phones and clothes are covered. I have heard of and witnessed boyfriends and girlfriends disappearing like the magician's assistant when the money runs out or a better, younger offer comes along.

Many tourists in this situation can be at least 30 years older than their Cuban partner. Foreign women, mostly Canadian and European, have a tendency to be attracted to tall, dark and handsome younger guys, whilst the older men seeking younger women are a mix of old decrepit Canadians, large Russians and dire horny Italians.

A friend commented that there is nothing more obvious than being introduced to "the boyfriend", a handsome younger guy with a large torso and even larger shoulders but skinny chicken legs (many Cubans don't "dead lift" weights), only to be introduced to him again with a different woman a few nights later. I may have witnessed an increase of "holiday boyfriends" in recent years - or maybe it's just living here that makes me feel that way.

Cuban male youths are groomed in romance by their older brothers, friends, uncles and fathers (who show them Hollywood romance films) in order to serenade European and Canadian women; it is like an entry into manhood for them. A wise person said, "if it's too good to be true, it probably is." This is likely to have been said by a woman!

So, straight prostitution unfortunately happens everywhere and it's the world's oldest profession. Not that this justifies the exploitation of those involved since prostitution has less to do with the act and more to do with control.

Visitors, tourists and travellers to Cuba could and do get the impression that prostitution is a big problem and getting worse with the increase of foreigners.

Living here I have a different experience to travellers, as you would expect. Yes, there is prostitution and it might be increasing, but I do not believe that it is at the same level as in other countries, such as the UK, France and US, where it is now conducted under the cover of the internet and mobile telephones. You only have to see in the news about websites bearing names like "Rich Sugar Daddies" to get an idea of what else is available via Google. In Cuba, it really is more of "demand and supply" then "supply and demand". I do not believe that Cubans enter prostitution due to destitution.

It could feel that prostitution in Cuba is a big problem, but I believe that this is only the case because it's more visible in everyday life and concentrated in a small demographic. Outside the tourists zones I have rarely witnessed it or been approached. Before individuals are convicted of soliciting or prostitution, there are multiple interventions from many social communities, associations and institutions, such as the FMC - Federation of Cuban Women (Spanish: Federación de Mujeres Cubanas) and CDR - Committees for the Defense of the Revolution (Spanish: Comités de Defensa de la Revolución). Only after multiple interventions have failed (including programmes whereby individuals are sent to other cities and towns and provided with training to gain new employment skills before returning to their communities) are people normally convicted. Unfortunately, there may be some inequality as these interventions tend to target women more than men, even though male prostitution is possibly more widespread in Cuba.

The situation I describe next seems to be mainly reserved for decrepit old Canadian and Italian men. This is about being seen in public in the company of a beautiful young Cuban woman, normally at dinner. Most men will speak no Spanish and the woman will refuse to speak any other language than her own - this is purely about getting a free dinner and not about sex or the company. This comes from the 1990s special period when food was limited.

After ordering from the menu, the woman will gaze around the restaurant at the roof, the walls, behind herself and out of the window (basically anywhere but at her companion), until the food arrives. Then they will eat quickly looking directly at the bottom of the bowl or plate. If a friend of the woman passes by the window of the restaurant, it is likely that they will be invited to join the "couple", resulting in a general catch up between the friends. Every now and then the women will smile and say "hola" to their dining companion and then giggle. As soon as dinner is finished the companion is thanked and the women will leave the restaurant alone.

A few years ago Cubans needed permission to leave the country. One of the ways to get out was to marry a foreigner, so befriending one and forming a relationship was popular in the past. The Cuban spouse would then proceed to disappear at the airport in their new country after "going to the washroom". Now this practice is a little out dated. I have met some men and women in Cuba and Europe looking for their spouses under these circumstances. Spouses living seemingly happy for a while from a few years to a decade and then leave without saying a word to anybody.

Internet & Email In Cuba

The sole provider for telecommunications in Cuba is ETECSA, which covers the internet, landline telephones and mobiles.

To fully appreciate the internet speed within Cuba, it's worth looking at the infrastructure that provides telecommunications services.

Until 2011, Cuba's internet speed was limited due to the use of satellite based infrastructure, which is slow and expensive to use and maintain. In February 2011, an undersea fibre optic cable was installed linking Cuba to Venezuela 1,600km (995 miles) away. This was funded by ALBA (the Bolivarian Alliance for the Peoples of Our America). It has been internationally recognised that Cuba's poor communication links with the outside world for the past 57 years have been due to the US blockade that has prevented the installation of a fibre optic cable to Florida just 90 km (955 miles) away. Internet services are available in most hotels I have visited across Cuba, including in one or two Casa Particulars, mostly from fixed computer points. Wi-Fi is also available in most hotels and in Wi-fi areas across the island - even in a hotel in the remote town of Baracoa. US-based ISPs and business and email services, such as Webmail, Hotmail, Outlook.com, Live, Yahoo and AOL are unlikely to work, but I have experienced better results sending and receiving emails from Yahoo Spanish addresses. I have used my Hotmail account many times successfully but the delivery and receipt of messages can be hit and miss. I recommend setting up a non-US-based email account before you go. For long-term secure email services, I recommend the Norway based Runbox, which will protect data by enforcing Norway's strong privacy regulations.

At the end of 2013 and the beginning of 2014, Habana-based hotels started applying conditions on the use of Wi-Fi services, which meant that only guests or residents of the hotel could use them. This was due, explained hotel staff, to the Wi-Fi infrastructure being unable to cope with the increase in demand. Unfortunately, some people's email is not web-based, which means they can only use Wi-Fi on their smartphones or laptops to receive messages. I encountered this particular scenario in the Hotel National. A US saleswoman was very frustrated as she had just started a new job and needed to ensure there were no outstanding requests on her email as she had left "everything to the last minute" before leaving for Cuba. She enquired if I was a resident at the hotel and tried to persuade me to purchase Wi-Fi time on her behalf. It is possible not to be a resident at a hotel and gain Wi-Fi time if you speak Spanish and smile. I explained to her that she should attempt to purchase Wi-Fi by claiming she was a resident. If there were any checks or questions she could claim she had only checked in a few minutes ago. A few weeks later I received an email thanking me for my advice - the young lady had successfully resolved the situation (see her email below).

Date: Jan 2014. Subject: Thank you! From: xxxx@xxxx.com To: Sasha
Hi Sasha
This is Sarah. Do you remember me? We met at the Hotel Nacional in Habana. I just wanted to thank you for your advice about getting Wi-Fi in Cuba, it really saved my job - haha! I went to Hotel Parque and followed your advice regarding finding an existing room number. When I went to purchase the Wi-Fi card, the lady did ask for my room

number and I gave it to her. She then checked the system and said that there was no one staying in that room, so I used the trick that you taught me and said that I had just checked in. She believed me and sold me a 5-hour Wi-Fi card, which I was able to use throughout my trip, even when I was in Varadero! Thanks a lot!
Sarah

Sarah has highlighted a fundamental point here: there is only one internet provider within Cuba so when you purchase an internet or Wi-Fi card you can pretty much use it within any internet cafe or place providing a Wi-Fi service that's frequented by travellers. If you travel outside of the norm, your experience may be different, but it's still possible and relatively easy to access internet services - just remember that Facebook stalking is not going to make you happy!

Cuban Women Of The Revolution

Many people say they have visited Cuba and others say they want to visit before it changes. People say they have heard of Che, Fidel and Raul; a few even know of Camilo Cienfuegos.

But outside of Cuba, few people around the world have heard of the Cuban women of the revolution, their achievements, or the making of a revolution within the revolution. The names Haydée Santamaria, Celia Sánchez Manduley, Vilma Espin, Melba Hernandez and Aleida March are widely unknown. Their pictures are not emblazoned on posters or on t-shirts, their insights regarding the revolutionary journey are not quoted in feminist journals or in schools or universities outside of the island of Cuba.

For me, these Cuban women are the most inspiring female revolutionaries in the 20th century. They displayed limitless commitment to social justice and tireless courage.

So why does the world outside Cuba not know about them? Well, most of them shunned the spotlight. They became revolutionaries not for the fame or for the glory, but to fight against tyranny. The other reason is the obvious sexism that plagues all the reporting of history, not just revolutions.

Haydée Santamaria was one of only two women who fought in the attack on the Moncada Barracks on the 26th July 1953 - the other was Melba Hernandez. Haydée's commitment even before this attack revealed tremendous courage and extraordinary self-sacrifice. Haydée ensured Fidel's escape from the attack by continuing to fight long after the plot had fallen apart. Haydée and her brother Abel were among those captured.

I learnt more about Haydée from my visit to the museum at the Moncada Barracks in Santiago de Cuba, which today is a school. (Following the triumph of the revolution all of Batista's garrisons or barracks were transformed into schools or education establishments.) Here, on the steps outside a class I read Fidel's recounting of Haydée's story that he told during the four-hour speech he made in court - History Will Absolve Me - following his arrest in the wake of the attack.

"A sergeant with seven other men, came with a bleeding human eye in this hand into the cell where our comrades Melba Hernández and Haydée Santamaria were held. Addressing the latter, and showing her the eye, they said, 'This eye belonged to your brother. If you will not tell us what he refused to say, we will tear out the other.' She, who loved her brave brother above all other things, replied with dignity: 'If you tore out an eye and he did not speak, neither will I.' Later they came back and burned their arms with cigarette butts until at last filled with spite, they told young Haydée Santamaria: 'You no longer have a boyfriend, because we killed him too.' And, still imperturbable, she answered: 'He is not dead, because to die for one's homeland is to live forever.' Never before has the heroism and the dignity of Cuban women reached such heights."

The torture and murder of her brother and boyfriend undoubtedly troubled Haydée for the rest of her life. She continued in the war as a tactician, gunrunner, international fundraiser, guerrilla combatant and coordinator of underground movements against Batista and his forces. In 1959, Haydée transformed herself from guerrilla to cultural emissary, wielding culture and art as the weapons for social change, that gave birth to the Casa de las Américas, under her direction.

Vilma Espin, was a chemical engineer, feminist and Cuban revolutionary. The daughter of a lawyer and from a wealthy background, she studied in Cuba and at MIT (Massachusetts Institute of Technology) in the United States in the 1950s. On returning from completing her post graduate masters studies, Vilma met with Frank

Pais and became a revolutionary. She would exchange messages with the 26th of July movement that had been relocated to Mexico by that the time.

Vilma was the president of the FMC, *Federación de Mujeres Cubanas* or Federation of Cuban Women from its foundation in 1960 until her death in 2007. Vilma donated her Santiago de Cuba home to the Federation that is still used today. The FMC had many aims for example to bring women out of the home and into the workplace or economy, remove women from subservient positions either in the home or workplace. Mobilizing women into political work and government administration as only women themselves could be trusted to provide equal opportunities for women. Also FMC was heavily involved in the 1961 Literacy Campaign and paved the way for the 1975 family code.

Melba Hernandez was declared "heroina del moncada" for she was one of only two women who fought at the Moncada Barracks assault in 1953 the other being Haydée Santamaría. Later in life Melba became a politician and diplomat to Cambodia & Vietnam. She served as Secretary General for the Organisation of Solidarity of the People of Asia, Africa and Latin America and in the National Assembly of People's Power in Cuba.

Aleida March was at the battle for Santa Clara in Las Villas and an active combatant in the Lightening Campaign in December 1958 that paralysed Batista's military forces occupying the province at the time. You can still see the derailed train carriages today in Santa Clara.

Others Have A Right-Hand Man, Fidel Had A Left-Hand Woman

Celia Sánchez Manduley was born on May 9th 1920 in a town called Media Luna, which now is in the province of Granma (named after the famous boat which was used by the revolutionaries in 1956 to cross from Mexico to Cuba).

Celia was an archivist, Cuban revolutionary, politician, landscaper and the left-hand woman of Fidel, as well as being an inspiration. Celia played a pivotal role in the Cuban Revolution and afterwards in the administration of the revolutionary government. She was one of the founders of the 26th of July Movement with Frank País - another very important member of the revolution. Travellers will see the flag of the 26th of July Movement as they travel around Cuba.

Around the world, Che Guevara is a household name, but Celia is little known outside of Cuba. Discovering the Cuban Revolution through Celia's life is both interesting and informative.

Celia and Fidel worked together before they met, exchanging covert messages with details of work to be completed. Once they had met it seems that they were inseparable. When I've asked Cubans if there was any romantic relationship between Celia and Fidel they say, "we all know they were very close" and smile and shrug their shoulders. As a Cuban friend once told me, nobody knows the truth but them. Celia and Fidel lived together in Habana and also adopted children in the early 1960s.

Celia was responsible for coordinating the South West coastal region of Cuba for the Granma landing and for arranging reinforcements once the revolutionaries had landed. She was truly courageous and served as a messenger, organised the installation of a telephone system across the Sierra Maestra and took part in radio broadcasting. She was one of the first women to assemble and join a combat squad, fighting with rebels deep in the Sierra Maestra and living at "Comandante la Plata" - the HQ of the revolution.

She collected documents that would later form the official archives of the Revolution and afterwards worked on many projects that enriched the lives of Cubans. These included architectural and design projects in Habana, such as the Coppelia ice cream parlour and Lenin Park. Celia was the driving force behind Cuba's most profitable exported cigar - the famous Cohiba!

See a short YouTube film about Celia's work here: https://youtu.be/z-YMYvn47pk

To find out more about Celia and the Cuban Revolution, I highly recommend Nancy Stout's book, "One Day in December: Celia Sánchez and the Cuban Revolution", which involved ten years of original research to complete. The author was initially barred from the official archives but in an unexpected twist was granted access by Fidel Castro himself.

You can read Alice Walker's foreword from the book here.

http://monthlyreview.org/2013/02/01/celia-sanchez-and-the-cuban-revolution/

Alice Walker is the author of the critically acclaimed novel The Color Purple, for which she won the National Book Award and the Pulitzer Prize for Fiction.

Women Travellers In Cuba

(by Emma O'Brien)

Many people have asked me: "Why do you like Cuba?" They question why I would want to live in a socialist country with no food on the grocery shelves, humid and hot weather, cockroaches the size of small ponies and an overabundance of macho Latino men.

Sometimes I find myself asking the same question. I am nearing nine months of living in Habana and somehow my love for this place persists and has deepened, although my patience has certainly been tested. To be realistic, there are good and bad things about every place in the world.

It is important to have the good outweigh the negative, and in my opinion it is helpful to live in a place that keeps you interested and makes you feel alive.

I'll be honest, after having no running water for the third time this week and showering with a water bottle, I crave the luxuries of the outside world. Doing my laundry by hand does not make me feel connected to the olden days. It is tiring and hard. I am glad that I know a Cuban family who offer to help me do my laundry in their machine every few weeks, but in the meantime I get to experience life without the convenience of technology. When I get to use the washing machine I feel like I could kiss it - it is such a wonderful invention.

Going to the stadium in the evening and playing pick-up soccer with an odd mix of foreign students and Cuban kids from the neighbourhood is a moment of true happiness. Spending the day on the beach with friends is paradise – there's warm water to swim in and palm trees to provide shade. I also love that every party always ends in a dance party.

It's frustrating when the electricity goes off for hours on end for no reason, and it gets unbearably hot without air-conditioning or fans. But the moment when the entire neighbourhood cheers when it comes back on again is a reason to smile.

Habana runs out of eggs for weeks, and I have to buy them from the black market. All anyone can talk about are eggs, and I have to hide my carton on my walk home so as not to cause a riot for groceries. I had a nice conversation with the egg man and now he gives me a giant hug every time I pass by. I find it entertaining that he works at the dairy store with no t-shirt on. I have a hard time imagining that being accepted in any supermarket in the United States.

Cheese is also an elusive item, and I dream of brie and smoked gouda at night. The man who has a fruit cart at the end of my street gifts me mangos, bananas and guyaba on my way home from school. The other day, a waiter in a restaurant saw me walk by and got the urge to talk to me. He walked out of the restaurant, in the middle of serving tables, with his apron still on and accompanied me down the street chatting. He was gone from work for almost twenty minutes and didn't seem the slightest bit fazed.

I love the old ladies who lean and chat from balcony to balcony about the latest neighbourhood gossip. I love my Cuban house mum who shouts "oh my god" after she sneezes and when her favourite songs come on. I love the street dogs who trot around and navigate traffic better than people do.

Watching the security guards at the Cuban wedding I was invited to was an amazing example of the Cuban work ethic. They began the evening very serious and intimidating. The first dance was to a Rihanna song, which was an odd choice because it was about terrible heartbreak, but nobody spoke much English so the irony was lost on them. The music came on and within one minute the security guards' legs began to wiggle. Another minute passed and one of them burst into full dance. He couldn't help himself and had to grab a lady and swing her around on the dance floor. By the end of the song, the security team was in the middle of the party having a great time. I managed to dodge the bouquet being thrown and catcalls flying through the air.

Understanding the term "machismo" and its significance in Cuban and Latin culture can be helpful in understanding why many Cuban men behave the way they do. Machismo plays a major role in creating the identity of men in Latin America. It is instilled in boys from an early age. Young boys begin to catcall, following the examples of their older brothers, uncles and fathers. Catcalling is a form of proving your manhood to others. Cuban women have told me that they are accustomed to these interactions with men in the street, and although not all women love them, they actually begin to wonder what is wrong with them physically if the streets are too quiet.

If a Cuban is interested in talking to you, they will not hesitate to come straight up to you. They will stare deeply into your eyes as you walk by.

Friends will tell you if you have gained weight. If you try to disagree, they will pinch your cheeks, arms and stomach to show you exactly where you've become fatter. Or else they'll look concerned and tell you you've lost weight and hand you something to eat. This type of directness is not delivered with negative intentions, but it often shows glaring differences between cultural notions of what might be appropriate to say to another person. Commenting on someone else's weight is the ultimate taboo in North American and European cultures, where there is great sensitivity around body image.

There is a different reality in Cuban culture. People seem to have fewer issues with body image and confidence. In fact, the amount of body confidence that Cubans have regardless of size or age is inspiring. There is no age or weight limit for women wearing Spandex leggings and sparkly t-shirts.

Sex tourism can be blatant, and it is not uncommon to see old foreign men walking around with one hand on their cane and the other wrapped around a young Cuban girl's waist. There are many middle-aged and older foreign women walking around in hot pants and short skirts with young Cuban men. In fact, there is an entire section of the Cuban population that makes a living from dating foreigners. The reality of the economic situation in Cuba is that anyone who has access to the tourist industry has a major advantage over those who rely on state wages, and many Cubans search for foreign partners in order to better their lives.

'Alone time' is a lost concept in my life, and I have adjusted my attitude towards privacy. I lived with a Cuban grandmother who would open the door while I was showering, even though there was no shower curtain. She'd chat with me about the prices of sandals and methods for making the best congris (a very typical Cuban dish of rice and black beans). She would shuffle around my room at all times of the day and night, sighing "Ayy Emmita." When she was feeling especially pleased with me, she would spray me with her favourite perfume and I would walk around for the rest of the day smelling like a sugar cookie.

Going to the bank takes an entire day. My friends studying medicine smoke more cigarettes than anyone else I know. The old man who leads ladies doing high kicks in an exercise class in the corner of the university stadium is more nimble than I was when I was 12. It's a good day when I don't run into public masturbation.

Watching sports on television with Cuban friends is a theatrical event with emotional reactions and passionate shouting that reaches all corners of the neighbourhood. I know every word to the theme song of my Cuban house mum's favourite telenovela. Internet is difficult to find, and my friends and family at home wonder if I am still alive. Social opportunities are abundant and early mornings are a thing of my past. I wake up to reggaeton blasting from my neighbour's stereo system and the smell of coffee on the stove… Habana bustles on.

Cuba Solidarity Campaigns, Groups and Networks

Solidarity for Cuba and the Cuban people stretches around the world, in the form of campaigns, groups and networks. These include the CSC (Cuba Solidarity Campaign) and Rock Around the Blockade in the United Kingdom, Support Cuba in Ireland, the CNC - Canadian Network on Cuba in Canada, Pastors for Peace/IFCO in the United States, Cuba Sí in Germany, as well as groups in Ireland, Belgium, France, Turkey, and Greece.

All these organisations offer diverse and wide ranging solidarity events, activities, Cuban history, information resources, ongoing news, brigades, tours of Cuba and cultural exchanges.

Most, if not all, of these organisations call for an end to the United States blockade against Cuba, and some campaign for their governments to oppose it. They believe it is up to Cubans to decide what's going to happen in Cuba without outside interference, such as from other people in their own nations.

For a long time there has been a call for the normalisation of diplomatic relations between Cuba and the United States. Some of the largest campaigns by these organisations were for the freedom of the group known as the Cuban Five, or the Miami Five, which you can read about in the chapter entitled "The Cuban Five".

Different groups offer different trips or tours. You can give your money to big commercial travel corporations or do something a little different, such as taking part in a Cuba Cycle Challenge. This is a wonderful way to see Cuba as you ride through hamlets, small villages, towns and cities. I've been told that the experiences you'll have with the local Cubans you'll meet as you ride will last a lifetime, and at the same time raise money for educational equipment for visually impaired Cuban school children. The money will also be used to support the work of solidarity campaigns and networks.

Brigades with young and old individuals offer the opportunity to participate in practical solidarity work by discovering the true reality of life for Cubans. This will provide a valuable insight into the many achievements of the revolution and the Cuban people. During the May Day Rally in Plaza de la Revolución in Habana, brigades from all over the world descend on Cuba. The people in the brigades get to witness the devastating effects of the United States blockade by meeting and discussing current issues with Cubans during visits to schools, hospitals, workplaces and neighbourhoods. In the past, brigades contributed to real work in agricultural and production areas. Today this is still available via voluntary work sessions.

Other tours, for instance the "Following Fidel Study Tour", include the same visits and meetings as the brigades but go deep into the Sierra Maestra, all the way to the Comandancia de la Plata, the camouflaged and remote HQ of the revolution. Here you will find

Che's Hospital, the bakery, the radio station, the press office and even a school.

Another option would be the "Viva Che Tour", where you'll get to meet Cuban doctors from the International Henry Reeve Brigade at Santa Clara Medical University. The tour includes educational visits to a Santa Clara children's foster home, the Literacy Campaign Museum and an organic urban agricultural co-op.

Other brigades and tours are available in the summer and winter for young trade unionists, environmentalists, educationalists and social workers.

The Pastors for Peace in the United States send "Caravans" to Cuba from US soil. These visit US communities on the way to explain their mission. Maybe you fancy this type of adventure!

Tours, brigades and events like these are exclusively arranged by solidarity groups and networks and cannot be booked via other commercial travel corporations, agents or tour companies.

I would encourage everybody to explore Cuba via a solidarity group or network arranged tour or brigade. Show solidarity by joining a group in your own country.

Ireland Solidarity

This group was established in 1991 because it was decided that Cuba was going to need friends in the world following the collapse of other communist countries. It was instrumental in lobbying the Irish government to first abstain on the annual vote on the blockade and then to vote against the US position. It organised a parliamentary pledge, which prospective members of parliament signed (and it held them to account when they were in government). In addition, it addressed the Joint Committee on Foreign affairs in 1992 to propose that Ireland should vote against the US position that year. Ireland abstained having previously done what the US wanted it to do.

The group set up the Free the Miami Five Campaign in 2002, lobbying government and civil society. This culminated in 47 members of the Irish parliament (out of a total of 166) and the former president, Mary

Robinson, signing an amicus curiae addressed to the US Supreme Court on its behalf.

You can see a list of its activities on its website: www.cubasupport.com and via Twitter: www.twitter.com/cubasupport

In addition, Ireland Solidarity is sending 20 organic gardeners to Cuba in January 2016 for a 10-day educational visit. Also, it will send two delegates to attend the forthcoming "Cuba Futures" event in London in October 2015. It hopes to live tweet from the event as we did with the 2014 international tribunal of enquiry into the case of the Miami Five.

The Canadian author, Keith Bolender will be visiting them in October 2015. Ireland Solidarity has hosted two speaking tours for his books Voices From The Other Side and Cuba Under Siege. Its late member, Bernie Dwyer, was a correspondent on Radio Havana Cuba for many years and the chief English language communicator for the Miami Five. Bernie has left a legacy of several excellent films on Cuba and on the Miami Five. Her final one was called The Day Diplomacy Died.

May Day 2016 – For All Travellers of around the world welcome!
Top Event – Check out the Cuba Wanderer Facebook Page for the event "May Day 2016 in Cuba International Workers' Day" for further details on marching the Cuban to Plaza de la Revolución. Bring your national flag!

http://ow.ly/ShgEi

Meeting at Address: Casa de la Amistad - Paseo Ave, No. 406, Entre 17 y 19, Vedado, La Habana, Cuba – At 07:00am, then marching to Plaza de la Revolución.

Solidarity Campaigns, Groups and Networks

Cuba Solidarity Campaign
c/o UNITE, 33-37 Moreland Street
London
EC1V 8BB
Britain
http://www.cuba-solidarity.org.uk

Cuba Support Group – Ireland
15 Merrion Square
Dublin 2
Tel: 087 6785842
http://www.cubasupport.com

Belgian Solidarity-Movement ICS
www.cubanismo.net   (In Dutch and French)

Germany   http://cuba-si.org

France
www.lesamisdecuba.com
http://cubacoop.org/

Canada
http://www.canadiannetworkoncuba.ca

United States
http://ifconews.org

Caravan Of Peace & Love

The Interreligious Foundation for Community Organisation (IFCO) - also known as the Pastors for Peace for short - has been working to bring an end to the US blockade of Cuba and has provided humanitarian aid to the Cuban people through Friendship Caravans, construction brigades and educational delegations.

The organisation travels through the US and Canada on prearranged visits to cities and communities participating in public events about the reality of life in Cuba.

The caravans or vehicles are normally brightly painted school buses that I have seen on the streets of Habana. But you won't just see the pastors in school buses, they also use trucks, ambulances, mobile libraries and cars, which are all packed with life-saving humanitarian aid donated by the people of Canada, Mexico and the US for the people of Cuba.

In 2015, IFCO sent its 26th caravan to Cuba. The first ever trip took place in November 1992, when 15 tons of simple humanitarian aid was carried by 100 "caravanistas". Items such as powdered milk, medicines, bibles, bicycles and school supplies were transported. The US government had never witnessed a direct grassroots movement against the blockade and IFCO reported that it responded with force. US treasury officers were filmed by CNN cameramen assaulting a Catholic priest who was carrying bibles to take to Cuba. This prompted thousands of calls to Washington and the caravan was allowed to cross the border. Reverend Walker, founder of IFCO Pastors for Peace, has said, "We act not just in defiance of our government, but in obedience to our conscience."

The IFCO is a great resource for information on Cuba from a progressive point of view. For more information, see its website: http://ow.ly/ShhrP

Also you can read a blog on the latest caravan here: http://ow.ly/Shhwu

The Cuban Five

Around the world there has been a steadily increasing desire for more details and information about the Cuban Five - who they are, why they were framed and when they were freed. I was at the University of Habana on 17th December 2014 when Gerardo Hernández, Ramòn Labañino and Antonio Geurrero arrived back in Cuba after 17 years in US prisons. René González and Fernando González had been released earlier, in 2011 and in 2014 respectively after spend 13 and 15.

The case of the Cuban Five is not that easy to explain, so it will take a little time as it's necessary to detail events in history in order to put the current situation into context.

So, were they just spies who got what they deserved? Or were they attempting to find information to prevent terrorism and protect people? Were they sent to infiltrate the military in the United States and steal classified material to pass on to rogue states (as largely claimed by groups in Florida)?

Well, more than 350 groups or committees in over 113 countries, a fair few hundred political organisations and thousands of individuals from across the globe worked for years to secure the men's freedom. You can watch for yourself the official documentary on the International Commission of Inquiry (English) on YouTube. It's narrated by Irma Gonzalez, daughter of Rene Gonzalez, and directed by the renowned Cuban director Roberto Chile. The film features all the witnesses who participated as well as guests, including former US Attorney General Ramsey Clarke, the author Alice Walker and the former head of the Cuban National Assembly, Ricardo Alarcon.

http://ow.ly/SizOq

For the Report of the International Commission of Inquiry into the case of the Cuban Five see:

http://ow.ly/SizYx

Cuba wanted to protect its right to self- determination, national sovereignty and independence, just like other nations. More importantly, Cuba wanted to prevent loss of life from terrorism, not just for its citizens, but for everyone.

After decades of experiencing terrorism and sabotaging actions, Cuba decided to try to prevent these types of activities. Since 1st January 1959 until today, the revolution has experienced aggression from armed counterrevolutionary groups that were originally organised and financed by former supporters of Batista, including property and business owners. Over the years and with increasing ferocity, more groups were established, mainly centred in South Florida where they could operate with impunity on the soil of the United States, with the CIA stepping into the former shoes of the financial provocateurs.

It has been widely reported that in over 50 years there has been close to 3,478 Cubans killed and 2,100 injured in 703 terrorist attacks initiated from the United States.

In the early part of the 1990s, 85% of Cuba's foreign trade was lost due to the collapse of the USSR. This resulted in a severe economic crisis referred to as the Special Period. The South Florida based counterrevolutionary groups were convinced that a domino effect would also see the demise of the Cuban revolutionary government, and they stepped up operations to assist with this transition.

Historically, the US government has looked for the demise of the revolutionary government and so created, changed or updated policies to encourage Cubans who were at the time hit by extreme hardship to sail across the Straits of Florida to the United States, mostly on dangerously flimsy boats and rafts, in the hope of what has become known as the wet foot/dry foot policy. Any Cuban found on the waters between Cuba and the United States would be sent back to Cuba and counted as "wet foot". Cubans that make it to the shore of the United States got the chance to remain - just one dry foot on the shore was needed to qualify. It is worth noting that this policy is designed specifically for Cubans.

Since 1959, there have been different types of steady and sustained activities, all with the same objective to remove the Cuban revolutionary government by any means possible. This has included the failed invasion of the Bay of Pigs, Operation Peter Pan, the 638 recorded assassination attempts or conspiracies to kill Fidel Castro, the failed attack in New York during Ché Guevara's speech at the United Nations, the United States blockade of Cuba, media smear campaigns, incursions of unauthorised planes into Cuban airspace, the terrorist bombing of a Cuban airliner and the terrorist hotel bombing campaigns that were designed to destroy Cuba's tourist industry.

In April 1961, Brigade 2506, a well reported and documented CIA sponsored paramilitary group, failed in the Bay of Pigs invasion. Over 1,400 paramilitaries organised into one paratrooper and five infantry battalions gathered in Guatemala before setting out to Cuba.

The former head of the Intelligence Directorate in Cuba claims that in 50 years or so there have been more than 600 plots and conspiracies to kill Fidel Castro.

In October 1976, a Cubana Airliner was destroyed over Barbados by two bombs on board the aircraft, killing all passengers, including 24 teenagers who were members of the national Cuban Fencing Team. They were returning home with medals won at a championship event. Declassified documents from 1976 highlight that the US State Department had concerns about the links between the CIA and extremist groups in the Cuban exile community. These point to Luis Posada Carriles as the most likely planner of the atrocity.

In the decade of the 1990s, there were multiple incursions of unauthorised planes into Cuban airspace by a group called Brothers to the Rescue (BTTR). These were portrayed as humanitarian missions to rescue rafters from the Florida Straits, but the reality of them was to provoke the Cuban military into shooting down unarmed civilian planes in order to receive military retaliation by Washington. In February 1996, two planes were shot down by the Cuban air force. The four pilots had refused to heed to warnings to turn back.

In 1997, Habana hotels and tourist sites experienced a string of bombings organised by counterrevolutionary groups. An Italian-Canadian businessman called Fabio Di Celmo was killed by a bomb planted in the Hotel Copacabana. Today in Habana there is a restaurant named in the memory of Fabio.

In April 1997, in the early hours of the morning in a nightclub located within the Hotel Melia Cohiba, a powerful explosion blew out a wall to a bathroom, smashing washbasins. About two weeks later, a hotel worker thought he might have found a suspicious device next to a lift on the 15th floor of the same hotel. On further investigation, a bomb was confirmed. The timing of this explosive device may not have been a coincidence as the following day was May 1st and many local people would have been marching directly in front of the hotel.

This was not the only device to be found around that time. Two children found one at the Commodore Hotel in Miramar. Nobody realised the danger posed by their discovery until around two years later.

In July 1997, bombs were detonated in the Hotel Capri and Hotel Nacional. The bomber had the audacity to hang about and watch the explosion that ensued.

In September of the same year, a man entered a bar at the Hotel Copacabana in Miramar, Habana, leaving behind a timed bomb in the toilet. He even had time to finish his beer before leaving. He continued to plant bombs in another three hotels and one in La Bodeguita del Medio, a famous bar and restaurant in old Habana. He returned to room 314 at the Hotel Plaza where the police later caught up with him. They were still questioning him at 11.00pm when the last bomb detonated – the man had said nothing during his interview to prevent it. He was sent Luis Posada Carriles.

Cuba believed that these sabotaging actions and acts of terrorism were being planned, managed and coordinated from Florida and Central and South American countries. In the 1990s, Cubans René, Fernando, Gerardo, Ramòn and Antonio started living in South Florida, having been sent there for intelligence gathering operations on counterrevolutionary groups planning violent attacks on Cuba, and on Cubans living within the United States and elsewhere. These five were not the only members of the intelligence gathering operation network, named the La Red Avispa (or The Wasp Network) - membership could have been as high as 27.

In June 1998, the Ministry of the Interior's security division, which was responsible for crimes such as espionage, sabotage and offences against Cuba invited the FBI to Habana. During this time they gave the organisation evidence collected by Cuban intelligence on past and future planned assassinations, bombings, attacks on Cubans and supporters of the revolution. It was reported that almost three months passed without any response from the FBI.

Between 1995 and 1998, FBI undercover surveillance of René, Fernando, Gerardo, Ramòn, Antonio and others began. The men's houses were secretly broken into and their files copied.

In September 1998, the FBI arrested 10 people, accusing them of being part of a "Cuban spying ring". Five of the arrested cooperated by spilling the beans to the FBI prosecutors, maybe telling them what they wanted to hear. The other five were René, Fernando, Gerardo, Ramòn and Antonio.

After being arrested, they were all denied bail. Instead they were held for 17 months in what are known as punishment cells, nicknamed the "hole". Each spent months in solitary confinement. Gerardo and Ramòn spent six months without company. In 2014 Cuban artist recreated "The Hole". An exhibit in Havana's Fine Arts Museum titled "No Agradezcan el Silencio" (Don't thank the silence) by artist Alexis Leiva Machado (Kcho). You can go in and experience it for five minutes like I did, see the pictures on my web site. (www.cubawanderer.co.uk)

In one of the longest trials in US history, all five men were convicted of all charges held against them. The trial was held in Miami, the home ground of most of the counterrevolutionary groups the men had been seeking information on. There were multiple motions for a change of venue to ensure they would receive an impartial jury or trial, but all of these were denied. It's been discovered that at the time of the trial, reporters received payments for writing articles against Cuba and the five men.

In December 2001, the men - now known as the Cuban Five - were sentenced. Gerardo was sentenced to two life terms plus 15 years, Ramòn to life plus 18 years, Antonio to life plus 10 years, Fernando to 19 years and Rene to 15 years. All were separated and taken to different federal prisons across the United States.

Since 2001, family members of the men were routinely denied visitation rights. Each of them were subjected to periods of solitary confinement – one for a period of just over a year. There were many appeals and new trials and in 2011 René González began a three-year probation period in the US and returned to Cuba in 2013. Fernando González was released and returned in February 2014, and the last members gained their freedom in December 2014.

For further information on the Cuban Five read "What Lies Across the Water" by Stephen Kimber. It is brilliant!

The Media, Newspapers & Magazines

Press freedom seems high on the agenda for everybody outside Cuba, but from my experience it's not that important to those within it. I've found over time that people talking about or visiting Cuba want to confirm what they have already decided about the country, and no amount of information will convince them to take a different perspective.

I have met, visited, interviewed and worked in different areas of the media within Cuba, so I have first-hand experience of it. I also have many friends that work at different media agencies and newspapers.

Find out for yourself, in Cuba or from home. For $50 a year you can get a subscription to Granma International from pathfinderpress.com.

Granma is printed in English, Spanish, French, Portuguese and (I believe) German. This version is the weekly international edition of the daily newspaper published by the Communist Party of Cuba.

http://ow.ly/SiAVn

Remember that there is a difference between the Communist Party of Cuba, the government and the state.

Alternatively, if you're on the streets of Habana, just pick up a newspaper.

Maybe the media is censored and closely controlled by the state, but is the rest of the world any different? The media is owned and control by a few people, just look at the Murdoch media empire. DA-Notice (Defence Advisory Notice), called a Defence Notice (D-Notice) before 1993, is a system still in use today in the United Kingdom. This is an official request to news editors not to publish or broadcast on specified subjects for reasons of national security.

Cuba Debate

An alternative information media that alerts about the defamatory campaigns against Cuba setup by students from Santa Clara University.

http://www.cubadebate.cu

Newspaper Titles

Trabajadores   published by the Centre of Cuban Workers
Granma   published by the Communist Party of Cuba
Juventud Rebelde   published by the Union of Young Communists

Regional Newspapers

Guerrillero	Pinar del Río
Tribuna de La Habana	Habana
Vanguardia	Santa Clara
Escambray	Sancti Spíritus
5 de Septiembre	Cienfuegos
Adelante	Camagüey
Periódico 26	Las Tunas
Ahora	Holguín

Cuba's Participatory Democracy

Cuba's system of local, provincial and national government has 169 Municipal Assemblies, 14 Provincial Assemblies and a National Assembly. In each area local people nominate and elect their Delegate to the Municipal Assembly who have to achieve 50% plus 1 of the votes to be successful. Cuba is divided into 16 Provinces, each with its own Provincial Assembly. They are made up of elected Delegates, up to half of them are Municipal Delegates. The National Assembly is the sole legislative body and is made up of 50% nominated delegates from mass organisations and 50% Municipal Delegates.

It is important to note that the Communist Party of Cuba is not an electoral party and is not allowed to nominate or stand candidates. Candidates are chosen by the people from amongst the people. Turn-out in the 2013 elections was 94% with 4.63% of papers blank and 1.2% spoiled ballots.

This is a very brief explanation of democracy in Cuba. I would recommend that you read Cuba's Participatory Democracy at http://ow.ly/SneiD

Best Night Life in Habana

El Diablo, Tun Tuń.

Looking for a local place to head to on a Thursday or Saturday night in Habana? Then go to what locals know as El Diablo Tun Tuń, and what tourists know as the Piano Bar. Oh wait, no, tourists don't come here!

Saturday night is live rock music and the crowd is young, highly educated, bright and very happy. Music in Cuba is not defined by the age of those listening but by the quality of what is being played. Remember, all Cuban ears have perfect pitch registers built-in, therefore only the best music and voices are recognised, appreciated and played. Cubans instinctively only listen to the best music. Musical genres move from Katrina and the Waves, to Rage Against The Machine and then to Metallica. Our own conceptual understanding of music may limit us, but not Cubans. Now I'm dancing to Jive Bunny with a room full of 20-somethings who not only think they are cool or hip by jiving and doing the twist, they are too, as they can really jive better than people in the 1950s - it is frustrating how good they are. The crowd is so energetic, so positive, so completely captivated and so in the control of the rock band gods playing. In El Diablo there are no limits on music, it's only you that holds back.

Avenue 35 between Calle 20 y 22, Miramar, Habana, Cuba

FAC Fábrica de Arte Cubano

Fábrica de Arte Cubano (F.A.C) holds a very special place in my heart. I love this venue and spend at least one night a week here. Why? Because there is nowhere else like it, whether that's in London, New York, Rome or Paris. Maybe, just maybe, Berlin could compete but that would be a stretch, a shot in the dark. It's located at the west end of Vedado before crossing the river into Miramar, but don't let that deter you from checking this place out. Not yet a tourist attraction, it offers the real deal, an authentic contemporary Cuban cultural scene.

This is a modern cultural Nirvana - a place of perfect peace and happiness. The concept of the venue beats any other because it is all done without any of the pretension that would accompany clubs in cities like Rome, London, NY and Paris.

La Fabrica has many possibilities, both indoor and outdoor: theatre, exhibits, drama, cinema, nightclub, live music, art gallery, fashion, design, a café and contemporary bars. You're not just visiting F.A.C, it is a life changing experience - it's buzzing with excitement, creativity and spirit.

I enjoy a cheap, killer strong Cuba Libre as I stroll around the white-walled maze-like area containing exhibitions and galleries, stumbling across small rooms on my way. There's a huge cinema screen upstairs and downstairs in the back hall I've listened to live bands play jazz, reggae/pop, punk and rock. I remember the night when I was the only British member of the audience at a tribute to the Beatles performed by over 10 different bands, but that was just one Monday night in 2014 - every one is different! We sit on furniture made from recycled materials and watch a play or re-enactment of why Celia Cruz left Cuba, a warts and all no censorship performance, either in the script or from the actors. We gather outdoors under the night sky or within a variety of intimate indoor spaces.

If it were not for Cuba I would never have found the jazz pianist Roberto Fonseca. If it were not for F.A.C I would never have witnessed the brilliant ability of percussionist Yissy Garcia and her band.

By the age of 25, Yissy Garcia had already become a leading iconic female figure in percussion in Cuba. She decided to launch her solo career as a bandleader of a new musical project that encompasses Latin jazz, funk and electronic music. Her session left me without words and a new identity with jazz.

For director X Alfonso, F.A.C is a labour of love with extremely talented curators and programming connoisseurs. It was a lifetime in the planning and is a quintessential multi-purpose factory of the arts, culture, music and poetry.

Part contemporary art space, part nightclub, it's mostly crowded and is set in a completely unique environment in which experimental moments can be shared with Cubans young and old, mostly young. Encounter works by artists of the future and witness contemporary dance and musical concerts that the rest of the world will have missed.

These days it's only open Thursday to Sunday, from 9pm, with live events not starting until 11pm.

It's best to arrive by Collectivo/Maquina and get there for just 10 Cuban Pesos. On Linea just before the tunnel (Calle 18 - 20) to Miramar and cross over Linea towards Calle 11 away from the Malecoń and turn right onto Calle 11 (towards Puente de Hierro) then walk a few blocks down to Calle 26.

There is a small cover charge on the way in - $2CUC or 50CUP – and in return you'll get a card. As you consume drink and food your card will be stamped. Don't lose the card! The maximum the card can hold is $30CUC before you are directed to pay and replace your card. You pay for everything upon exiting the establishment. If you lose your card you pay the maximum, which is $30 CUC.

On Calle 26, between Calle 11 & 13, Vedado.

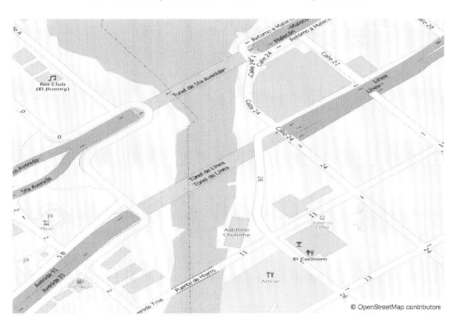

© OpenStreetMap contributors

Espacios - El Espacio

This venue is situated in Miramar, in the vicinity of F.A.C and El Diablo Tun Tuń. Espacio inserted itself into Habana's social scene a few years ago, and then it was only Cubans or Spanish speakers who knew about it. It was a venue for friends and artists, but now celebrities are spotted there too, mainly pretending to be part of the local scene only to fly away the next day. Where F.A.C and Diablo have no pretension, this place has oodles, mainly from the staff.

Until recently I had only ever visited Espacio late at night, or should I say in the early hours of the morning. There are multiple non-contrasting rooms where you instinctively tune into the vibe and wonderful food, which is expensive for Habana, but similar to Europe.

The outside look is so different to the inside. Set in a big mansion and a tranquil garden bar, it has not changed much over the years and it shows how good Habana can be. It's just a shame that more Cubans don't get to experience it. Wandering into the kitchen by mistake, I spent some time with the chef who seems to be influenced by cuisines from Japan, India, Spain and Peru. I spent the next hour in the kitchen tasting and experiencing great food by brilliant people who can cook and know about cuisine.

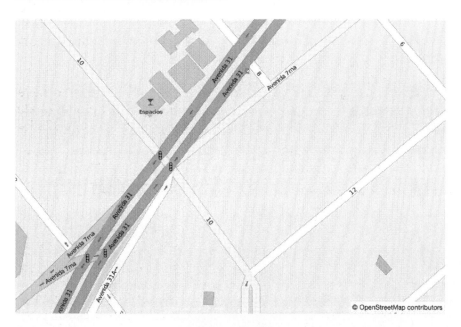

Calle 10 #513
entre Calles 5 y 7
Miramar, Playa, La Habana, Cuba
http://www.espaciosHavana.com

Bertolt Brecht

Don't' tell anyone!

If you are looking for traditional Cuba, a little salsa or maybe Buena Vista Social Club, then look elsewhere, this is not going to be your place. Otherwise, head down on Wednesdays and the rest of the week too!

I guess that this place is named after the German playwright, poet and theatre director, Bertolt Brecht. It is a cultural venue for everybody, young and old, and it attracts the best up-and-coming Cuban musicians and theatre productions.

It's maybe the second coolest nightspot now (after the opening of F.A.C) and though a main theatre takes up most of the space in the building, the place to be is the basement Café theatre. "No se lo a nadie" or Café Brecht, happens Tuesdays, Thursdays and Fridays. There's no real dance floor, though moving to the music is obligatory - not just here but anywhere in Cuba!

I've experienced very different energy and crowds here, and have seen some of the most beautiful people I've ever laid eyes on (male and female). At times it felt that being beautiful was a prerequisite for entry.

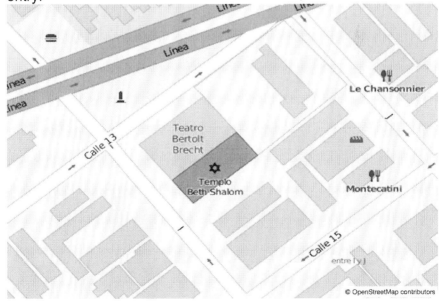

TaBARish

Around the corner from the Swiss Embassy, and just off 5ta Avendia (Fifth Avenue), we have TaBARish, a contemporary Soviet bar with historic memorabilia.

Remember, there is going to be a difference between Russian and Soviet styles. By the entrance there is a display of posters and advertisements from the Soviet period, but your attention will soon be pulled away by the bar - it is huge. It's a great place to hang out with friends, especially if you speak Russian! I come here for the great authentic homemade cuisine, and it is widely recommended for its octopus, katieti and pimiento.

Calle 20, Between 5ta y 7ma Miramar
+53 7 2029188

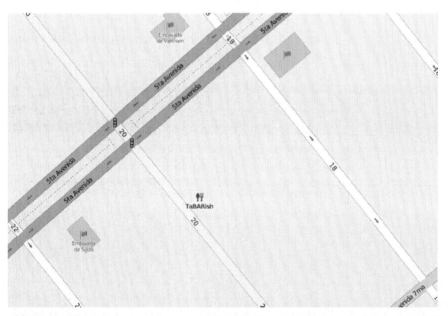

Up and Down

Up and Down is always packed at the weekends. The decor is sharp and normally there is a hardy atmosphere over two floors, with two cocktail bars. The top one is a VIP area. Watch out for the minimum $20CUC consumption per person – this is aimed and priced for foreigners. The bottom one is more for dancing and music. Also upstairs there is a super quiet place with very good service. If you are looking for an international wave of foreigners mixed with Cubans this could be the place for you. It is not a bad venue and I've had some enjoyable times downstairs. Calle 5ta y B, Vedado

Shangri-La

Located in Playa, Habana, Shangri-La offers cheap drinks and the entertainment is amazing. The bartenders are all handsome and fast and they put on a show while they make the drinks. The music is also awesome. The place is small and exclusive and the doormen can be surly and rude.

Address: 21 y 42, Playa.

Sloppy Joe's Bar

Situated on the corner of Calle Animas and Zulueta in Habana Vieja, Sloppy Joe's welcomed tourists for decades and offered over 80 different cocktails, before a disappearing US clientele and a fire in the 1960s finally finished it off. It reopened in 2013 after being closed for decades.

In the 1950s, I very much doubt if everyday Cubans could have afforded to be in Sloppy Joe's bar. It was a magnet for celebrities from the United States, as well as wannabe celebrity tourists. It was apparently described in the LA Times as "one of the most famous bars in the world" and 90% of the customers were from the US.

Today, the only change is that now the customers are 99% tourists from around the globe, and the prices reflect this, but do go and see the restoration. You'll find memorabilia from the time and experience the arctic air conditioning they had back in the1950s too!

But now that Sloppy Joe's is a tourist trap (funded by the Cuban state) and only designed with them in mind, I'm deeply embarrassed and ashamed of what it has become. I will never be seen inside again. This is not Habana, this is not Cuba, it's just a transplanted bar from London, Paris or Rome.

Submarino Amarillo (Yellow Submarine) Club

Even though the Beatles never visited Cuba, Beatlemania is still huge in Cuba today. John, Paul, George and Ringo would be astounded at how much Cubans love their music.

The Submarino Amarillo is on the corner of John Lennon Park in the heart of Vedado on Calle 17 y Calle 6. It opened in 2011 and is often very crowded with nightly shows from around 10pm. Arrive early for a table or it will be standing room only. The cover price is around 50CUP for locals, so maybe $2 - $5 CUC, depending on the band. Get the deal from the menu, a bottle of rum, four TuKolas (Colas) and ice for less than $10CUC, but always upgrade to dark rum (Añejo Especial) - you will thank me in the morning. Alternatively, try the club's special drink, Submarino Amarillo. My preference for going is on Friday's after I've been "working like a dog".

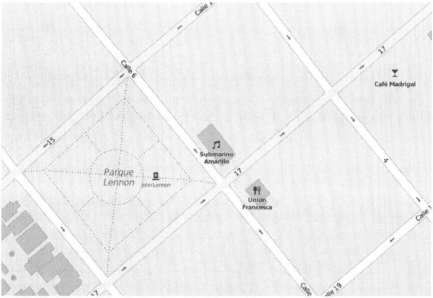

John Lennon Park, Calle 17 y 6, Vedado

1830

Apparently 1830 is a restaurant, but I only found out this a few months ago. Since then I've eaten very good food at this superb and elegant colonial house, which has excellent service. It's worth visiting and dining there but really I go for the salsa at night!

It's outside so watch out if it is raining. If you dance salsa and want to shake your ass then come and show us what you're working with.

Situated at the end of the Malecòn, tourists are bussed in en masse on Sundays, which is not as bad as you might think, with crowd participation in line-ups and live bands that even after years I still enjoy, even if it is a little repetitive.

Student friends from Habana University attend on Thursdays – this is our dance night! Be sure to arrive after 10:30pm and don't go on Fridays or Saturdays.

The cover is $2-3CUC and rum is getting expensive - around $15CUC for a bottle. Buy as a group and share.

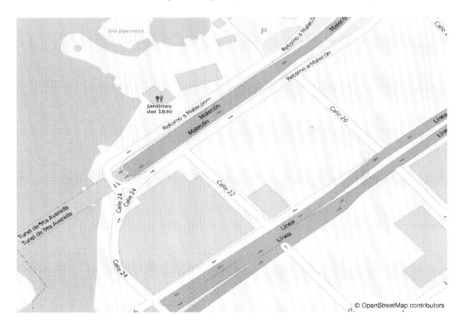

© OpenStreetMap contributors

La Grutra

HOT Salsa set in a basement that feels like a cave, this is the place to see late night salsa (11:00pm) Wednesdays are the best! This is the serious dancing establishment with live salsa shows by professional dancers, although the locals are better. This place is frequented by Cubans and only people in the know!

On Calle 23 - Entre O y P

Humboldt

Waking up slowly, I can hear the end of a karaoke song and the start of a drag performance. Now I'm awake. Where am I? In Humboldt #52 between Hospital and Infanta, Central Habana / Vedado. Regardless of your sexual orientation, this place has a welcoming vibe, a relaxed setting and a great dance floor for salsa. Like most gay bars in the world, there is a disco ball and my friend returns from mistakenly entering the 'back room"!

There's seating aplenty and big TV screens show music videos, making this a fun place for a night out. I'm somehow reminded about a distant memory of dancing in G.A.Y in London to Glee Cast's Don't

Stop Believin' and being asked to desist as dancers don't mix with the clientele, there should be nobody dancing better than clientele, its just unfair.

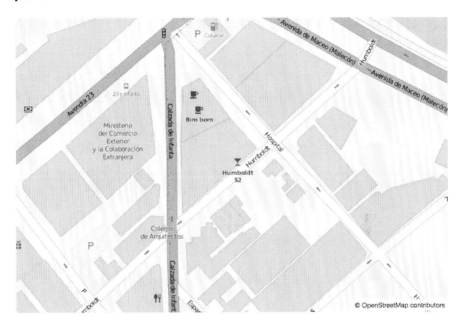

Fashion Bar Habana

Fashion Bar is located in Habana Vieja on San Juan de Dios, Esq. a Aguacate. I used to visit this venue with friends from Europe - we went on Saturdays and it seems the place reinvents itself pretty regularly, new cuisine and "cock"tail surprises are in store! The decor is 1920s or 1930s although I'm no expert.

Las Vegas

I discovered this venue walking down Infanta between Calle 25 y 27 Vedado, near to La Rampa. It's well established and some accomplished drag acts perform there. I met many wonderful people and enjoyed strong drinks and great music. The restaurant on the end of the block is excellent too.

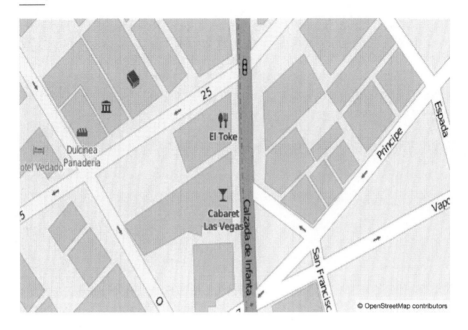

Cafê Bar Madrigal

LGBT friendly Cuban bar for folks 25 plus. This is a place for those who don't like their music too loud and prefer a comfortable seat. The atmosphere mirrors the San Francisco vibe and the music is cool. However, it didn't have the atmosphere our group was looking for, but maybe that's due to our age - most people will like this place!

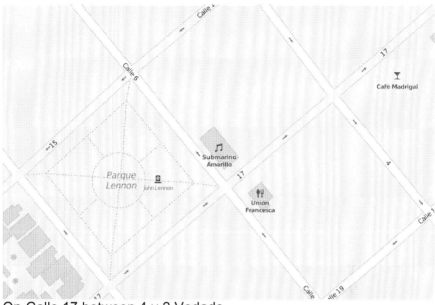

On Calle 17 between 4 y 2 Vedado

Escaleras al Cielo

In Habana Vieja, on Zulueta 600 between Apodaca y Gloria, and displaying another disco ball, Escaleras al Cielo is a spot where LGBT Cuban youth go on Fridays to show their groove and a laser light system leading all the way up a stairway to heaven.

Bar Bohemio

Situated in Vedado, Bar Bohemio is more restaurant than bar. It's housed in a mansion, has a lounge style bar, excellent service and the friendliest waitress I've met in a long time. There's also a laid back atmosphere, with tasty tapas at reasonable prices.

Living here has made me an expert in all things rum: Mojitos, Cuba Libres and Pina Coladas. Bohemio is maybe the best place for them - not just in Habana, but in the world!

Calle 21 between 12 y 14 Vedado

Bolabana

This place is so pretentious until you speak to the beautiful young Cuban crowd. They are trying to act cool without knowing that they don't need to - if I keep returning to Bolabana I will fall in love with a member of staff or a customer!

Calle 39 esq 50, Playa

Getting out of Habana

This is easier said than done, but you have more options than you think. A Víazul coach appears to be the default option for many, but you should consider taking the Hershey train from Casablanca just over the harbour to Matanzas. You can also leave by truck or Camións, or a Maquina Colectivo Taxi, from either Habana train station or the Omnibus National Station. Depending on your timescales and departure point, it is worth flying down to Santiago de Cuba. In December 2013, I booked a flight there for the following week. It cost $120CUC, but prices normally start at $75CUC. The most I have ever paid, and this was for a flight leaving the following day, was $170CUC. More recently it's been necessary to book flights well in advance, so you will need to do some forward planning if you want to fly. The choice is 15 hours on a Víazul coach or 90 minutes on a plane to Santiago!

From experience, Viazul provides a punctual and reliable service and should not be compared with coach services from other nations. This is because you're not in another country - you're in Cuba!

Unfortunately, Viazul coaches in popular locations, such as Habana, Trinidad and Santiago de Cuba, tend to get oversubscribed as demand is high. This can get frustrating. In Habana between March and June 2015, seats for express Viazul coaches were fully booked four to five days in advance, and internet bookings via its website weren't honoured.

I have managed to purchase a ticket on board a Viazul without booking in advance, however, I was either traveling alone or in a pair; I doubt this would work for a group. In the near future everyone will have to book in advance.

It's a pain to have to go out to the Viazul station just to make a booking, so use a Maquina/Colectivo from Calle 23 or from xxx, then visit the zoo next door or walk back to Calle 23. You'll experience a part of Habana you wouldn't normally see so take a camera, there are some great authentic shots to be had.

Booking A Flight
Head to what looks like a bookstore opposite the Capitolio in Habana Vejia on the corner of Calle Teniente Rey. Go inside and you will see the flight desk to your left.

Maquina/Colectivo City to City

Head to the Omnibus National Station near Plaza de la Revolucion - on Avendia de la Independencia - Between or entre C19 de mayo y Bruszon.

Upon entering the station from the main front entrance on Avenida de la Independenica, turn right and head towards C19 de mayo. You need to negotiate the rate to your destination, and either pay the same as you would for a Víazul bus or less. Your journey will be quicker than the coach and not as cold.

Otherwise, if you don't mind travelling by truck, head to the train station in Habana Vieja. Trucks leave throughout the day and night but plan your journey so you avoid travelling in the middle of the day; it's really not pleasant.

For People With A "Carne"

As I hold a "Carne" (a temporary residence of Cuba) I am entitled to use Omnibus National Coaches, which are much cheaper and reliable. However, journey times are long as they stop in lots of different places. Individuals who do not hold a Carne are normally prevented from using Omnibus National services because Viazul is designed to accommodate travellers and tourists. You won't get on an Omnibus unless you have a Carne or speak Spanish and smile. I use them for journeys with friends or when I have time on my hands and don't need to be at my destination at any particular time.

My best experiences while travelling through Cuba have been on tucks, in Maquinas and on Omnibus coaches.

Víazul - From Habana

I have travelled many times across Cuba using Viazul, so I have a lot of experience of these coaches to share with you.

Bring warm layers. Like most buses in Latin America they get very cold, especially if you intend to sleep. Many of the toilets in terminals require paying for and they do not have change. Bring lots of coins and plenty of tissues.

Bring some the food and water with you for the entire journey. Most terminals have a little food or drinks for Habana and Santa Clara well resourced. For example, if you do the trip from Baracoa to Trinidad via Santiago de Cuba it's a 16-hour journey with limited stops and short time for food. Casa hosts are often happy to pack you a meal for the trip.

Familiarise yourself with fares and timetables listed on the official Viazul website, ideally before you arrive in Cuba. http://ow.ly/ShhWz

Habana University - Language and other Courses

On 17th July 2015, 25 foreign students, making up 16 nationalities, graduated after completing their studies at Habana University. They had spent almost six years in Cuba. Together they recalled their passage through student life and shared their expectations about the future. The graduates expressed their deep gratitude to the university and the people of Cuba for their hospitality, training and love. They also stated their commitment to becoming ambassadors of the university (and Cubans) back in their home countries.

Habana University and others throughout Cuba are open to people from all over the world. ELAM (Latin American Medical School) is an international medical school where students are taught free of charge. Find out more in my chapter about ELAM. Meanwhile, the Spanish department of the Faculty of Foreign Languages offers intensive language courses. The faculty has over 30 years' experience in the practical application of teaching Spanish.

The courses are available to anybody interested in learning or improving their Spanish language. The professors within the faculty are amazing and wonderful individuals. They are highly dedicated, motivated and professional and are a true credit to the university and their families. Having them in my life has made me a better person, and I've learnt more than a second language – I have learnt about how to be a better human being, how to feel and how to see more in the world around me.

I have met students from between the ages of 18 to 76. They have been Palestinian, Dutch, Turkish, Slovakian, German, Italian, Japanese, Canadian, Scandinavian, French, Korean, Chinese, Irish, Scottish, Russian and Australian (plus there has been a few British and US people).

In my time at the university I found the students to be very inclusive - regardless of an individual's ability to speak Spanish - when arranging or organising activities after lessons and at the weekend.

You will have a brilliant time studying there.

Short Courses

Enrolment in short courses happens on the first Monday of each month, except August. On this day students enrol on the course and their appropriate level is determined. Don't worry - this is not as scary as it sounds.

At 9am there is a presentation explaining the courses available and the necessary information such as times, length and costs. These are spoken in Spanish and English.

After the presentation, you will be asked to complete a Spanish written test. Most of you will write your name clearly on the top of the test paper and then look around the room. Don't worry if you have no written Spanish, just smile and the staff will notice and direct you to the next stage - the oral test. Oh no! Others will be sitting next to you scribbling away. Again, don't worry about them.

Most of you will enter the oral test room and say maybe Hola or something you believe could be Spanish. Others will be pretty fluent. Again, don't worry – everyone is there to learn.

When you have finished your oral test, you should be directed to fill out your application enrolment form - don't leave the building before doing this. The application form requires personal details such as your name, passport number, nationality, D.O.B., address in Cuba and home address, plus emergency contact details. Write in BLOCK CAPITALS, you will see why when you receive your contract.

TOP TIP

You will need two passport-sized portrait photos of yourself. Depending on the length of your course you will need between 2 and 10 photos. You can get these in Cuba, but it would be better to take them with you. Locations of Photo ID services are listed further down in this chapter.

TOP TIP

I recommend getting between two and eight full colour or black and white copies of your passport, just for the university.

Apart from the months of December, April and July, four-week courses are available. Be aware of Easter in 2016 and 2017 as the courses in March/April may be split into two parts, with a week's holiday in the middle. Pay attention to the months that have five weeks in them as the courses are likely to be unpredictable.

Levels

Beginner - Principate
Elementary - Elemental
Intermediate - Intermedio
Advanced - Avanzado
Top - Superior

Costs and Packages

Short Courses

Duration	Price
One Week	$100CUC
Two Weeks	$200CUC
Three Weeks	$240CUC
Four Weeks	$300CUC

(I don't know why week three is only $40CUC more, but this is correct.)

Duration	Price
Four Months	$960CUC
Six Months	$1392CUC

Short Courses - Lengths & Timetables

The first Monday of the month is always enrolment so there are no teaching sessions. After enrolment has finished the rest of the day is free.

To make up for this short Monday, hours are extended over the next four days. For the rest of the month lessons are spread out over five days.

Week One   **Tuesday - Friday**
1st Class: 9am -10.30am
Break: 10.30am - 11am
2nd class: 11am - 12:30pm
Break: 12.30pm – 12.35pm
3rd Class: 12.35pm – 1.30pm
Ends

Weeks Two, Three and Four   **Monday - Friday**

1st Class: 9am – 10.30am
Break: 10.30am – 11am
2nd Class: 11am – 12.30pm
Ends

Long Courses

There is the opportunity to study Spanish over a longer period of time. Courses begin in September and end in July. They alternate between three and two day weeks.

There are two different types of long courses: the academic term that is for anybody and the preparatory course, which is really designed for students who have completed high school and arrive in Cuba to pursue courses at the university in the next academic year.

Costs: academic term: $1798CUC. Preparatory course: $2000CUC

There are other courses available too. These are:

Integral Practice Spanish Language I $500CUC
Integral Practice Spanish Language II $400CUC
Course in Cuban Culture (of around 60 hours) $360.00 CUC

For more details, check out the university's website, or you could try emailing Alexeis. He's a great guy but don't worry if you don't receive a reply from him, just turn up on the first Monday of the month and you will be fine.

Office of International Academic Services
Alexeis Baez Sanchez
alexeis@rect.uh.cu
Phone: (537) 870 46 67
http://www.uh.cu/cursos-de-espanol

You can study for up to either 2 months or 6 months, depending on your tourist visa and/or if you've exchanged your tourist visa for a student one. You can do this after you have arrived in Cuba - there is no need to prearrange. In fact, it is harder to arrange it beforehand.

If you apply for a student visa you will need to purchase stamps from the bank. Don't worry, this is easy and straightforward, if you are organised.

Check with Daniela or Alexeis in the office about the current stamp values needed for a student visa.

For three and four months - stamps value $40CUC.
For six months – stamps value $50CUC

Your tourist visa will be exchanged for a "Carne de Identidad" and you will be granted the status of "Residencia temporal". How Cool!

You will need to visit an immigration office, which will be arranged for you, as you will have to sign your "Carne" directly. Also, you will have your thumbprint taken and your height confirmed in centimetres.

Paying For Your Course

In week one, on the Tuesday or Wednesday, you should receive in your classroom your contract, which will state the length and cost of your course.

Check this carefully, especially the spelling of your name, nationality and passport number. If incorrect, get this changed in the first break or at the end of the lesson. Do not delay or wait until tomorrow.

Check all the contract details match your course length and cost. If incorrect, do not put off getting this changed.

You pay for your course on the Thursday or Friday of the first week. This is normally done in the classroom next to the administration office, where the wonderful and ever helpful Daniela is located. When your lessons end around 1.30pm this will be your only opportunity to pay at this location.

This process is long, or the queue will be long, depending on the number of students. Try arranging with your professors to finish early so you can be at the front of the queue. Tell the people behind you that you learnt this from my book!

Normally, there are between two or three students in the payment room at any one time - I have known it to take over two hours for everybody to be seen.

If any mistakes or incorrect paperwork are found, you will be unable to pay on this day. New paperwork will need to be printed on the following day and you will be required to make the payment in person at the Directorate of Economics at the University of Habana, in a building that's around a 45 to 60 minute walk from where the Spanish lessons take place. Now you should be clear on why you need to be organised and write your enrolment application form in clear BLOCK CAPITALS.

Unfortunately, the university contract and the payment part of your course are entered on two different systems, so sometimes payment paperwork does not match the contract paperwork, which is out of your control. Again, you will not be able to continue with the payment process that day. But don't worry, this happened to me.

Just go for an ice cream! After living in Cuba for a while some of us at the university developed a Spanish saying whenever anything like that happened - "Esta es Cuba", but we were always smiling.

The Directorate of Economics is located on Calle 13, Entre 8 and 15 in Vedado, in a big white house on the corner. The building does not have any signs or markings. It is open between Monday and Friday. Go early before class (around 8.30am) and wait. I do know they are open in the afternoons, but I cannot keep up with the changes so ask fellow students who have been around for a while.

You will need to make the payment in the next few days as you will not be able to join future lessons until payment is made in full. This policy is currently fairly relaxed and I have known it take some students up to a week to pay, but they still attend lessons in the meantime.

Where To Eat, ID-Photos, Miscellaneous.

Be quick about eating – you only have 30 minutes.

There is a cafeteria in the grounds of the university. Directions are hard to explain so see the map below. It serves juices, large sandwiches and snacks, accepting payment in National Pesos.

On Calle Ronda next to the university (east), between San Miguel and Neptuno, is a well-known and lovely cafeteria serving coffee, yoghurt and a range of sandwiches. These are all sold in National Pesos out of a window, which is normal.

On the west side of Habana University there is Calle J, between Jovellar y Calle 25, which is littered with Cuban local cafeterias and paladares. These serve everything, including pizza and cake, again all sold in National Pesos.

ID Photos

There are many places in Habana that offer photographic and printing services, one of the easiest places is near to the University on Calle L - between Calle 25 and 23 - directly opposite the Habana Libre Hotel. Also on Calle 23, between J and H, look for the signs of cameras and printers.

Drinking Water

To the best of my knowledge, there is nowhere to buy bottled drinking water at the university. See my section on the water filter bottle that you should purchase before arriving in Cuba. It will save you time and money.

Dictionaries

For those students arriving in Cuba without a dictionary, don't worry. An excellent Spanish School dictionary can be purchased. This is better than other dictionaries as it includes verb tables. At the bottom of the steps of the university on Calle L, diagonally opposite Hotel Colina, there is an excellent bookshop where you can purchase this Collins Spanish to English School Dictionary (there's also Spanish to other languages). The School Dictionary can be found in the glass display cabinets, as well on the bookshelves.

Maps

Maps of Cuba, road atlases and local maps of cities are available on the island, or via the internet. For driving I would use the "Carreteras De Cuba" - see the picture above.

Habana Vieja

To see a good selection of maps head down Obispo Street, to the window directly on the corner of San Ingacio, opposite the Café Paris. See the map below for the exact location.

Habana Vedado

Another great place for maps would be directly on the corner of Calle 27, opposite the Hotel Colina, in the bookstore known as Librería Fernando Ortíz. When inside head for the left far corner, near the windows.

You will find links to local maps of cities throughout Cuba on my website under the blog entitled Maps. In order to get the image to fit your printer settings, make sure you "scale to fit" just before you print.

Pope Francis Visits Cuba, September 2015

On 19th September 2015, Pope Francis will arrive in Habana, Cuba. He is expected to tour the island with President Raul Castro and will celebrate Mass in three different cities: Habana, Holguin and Santiago de Cuba. Pope Francis is expected to deliver his first sermon of the trip celebrating Mass in Habana's Plaza of the Revolution. Thousands of people are expected to attend.

Bishops in Cuba released a statement saying: "The Holy Father wants to show us how important this moment is for him...Thanks in part to his mediation, our country has a new breath of hope as a result of the new possibilities created by the dialogue taking place between the United States and Cuba."

In 1973, Fidel Castro predicted in the international press that the United States would come to talk to Cuba when it had a black president and the world had a Latin American Pope.

Pope Francis's visit follows other trips made by Pope John Paul II in 1998 and Pope Benedict XVI in 2012. All three popes have repeatedly called for an end to the US blockade of Cuba.

Raul and Francis met privately in May at the Vatican. Afterwards Raul reported that he was so impressed with the discussions that he was considering returning to the church.

It is anticipated that the Pope will urge Raul to allow the reopening of Catholic schools in Cuba. However, education in Cuba is secular therefore any alterations would need a change in Cuba's constitution by mass consultation and support of the population. The Argentinian Pope has been a popular figure in Cuba, though recent surveys did indicate as many as 50% of Cubans do not consider themselves religious.

On Monday 21st September 2015, Pope Francis will bless and celebrate Mass in public at Cuba's fourth largest city, Holguin, then continue to Our Lady of Charity at El Cobre, near to Santiago de Cuba.

The following day he is intending to meet with local Cuban families in Santiago de Cuba and celebrate Mass in the city's Central Plaza.

In the past, Pope Francis has been known to deviate from schedules and he frequently stops to speak with people on the streets - the Cuban tour should be no different. Previous pope visits have been broadcast live on Cuban television, and the same is expected this time.

	19th September 2015
10:15 a.m	Departure from Rome's Fiumicino airport to Havana.
4:05 p.m	Arrival ceremony at Havana's José Martí International Airport.
	20th September 2015
9 a.m	Mass In Havana's Revolutions Square
4 p.m	Visit with Cuba's President Raul Castro in Havana's Place of the Revolution
5:15 p.m	Celebration of vespers with priests, religious and seminarians in Havana's Cathedral.
6:30 p.m	Greeting to young people at the Father Felix Varela cultural centre in Havana
	21st September 2015
8 a.m	Departure by air to Holguin
9:20 a.m	Arrival at Holguin's Frank Pais International Airport
10:30 a.m	Mass in Holguin's Revolution Square
3:35 p.m	Blessing of the city of Holguin from Cross Hill
4:40 p.m	Departure by for Santiago de Cuba
5:30 p.m	Arrival at Santiago de Cuba's Antonio Maceo International Airport

7 p.m	Meeting with bishops at the seminary of St Basil the great in El Cobre.
7:45 p.m	Visit to Shrine of Our Lady of Charity of El Cobre
	22nd September 2015
8 a.m	Mass in the Minor Basilica of the Shrine of Our Lady of Charity of El Cobre
11 a.m	Meeting with families in the Cathedral of our Lady of Assumption in Santiago de Cuba and the blessing of the city
12:15 p.m	Farewell ceremony at Santiago de Cuba's International Airport.

Travelling To Cuba Over The Last 17 Years

Believe you are too old to travel around Cuba? Well, age does not stop Brian and Mavis Clarke from doing it, and they are both in their 70s!

Here's what Brian has to say...

My wife Mavis and I first visited Cuba in 1998. We had friends who had been going there since the mid 1960s and took groups from South Yorkshire. The idea of a holiday in Cuba had interested me because being a Socialist I wanted to see first-hand what the Socialist island was really like. We were not disappointed. We had a split holiday, flying into Habana for two days, then taking a flight to Holguin for 10 days and staying in Guardalavaca, a beach resort, then back to Havana for another two days before flying home. Of course, in 1998 Cuba was still in what they called "The Special Period" and due to the fact that the Soviet Union was no more there were many shortages of food and general domestic necessities. Also, the government was no longer getting cheap oil/petrol from the USSR so there were few cars on the roads. Through our friends, Eddie and Marion, we met several Cuban families and visited a couple of hospitals, farms and schools. Wherever we went the welcome was fantastic and even though many families had very little, they were happy to share what they had.

Since 1998, we have probably visited the island 15 times and have travelled to many cities, from Santiago de Cuba in the east to Pina del Rio in the west. We have made many friends along the way. Most of our holidays have been package ones, but more recently we have travelled independently, staying in casa particulars. This has given us a better understanding of the day-to-day life of ordinary Cubans.

In 2005 our whole family went to Cuba to celebrate my 65th birthday, which was spent with Cuban friends on their farm close to Guardalavaca. Our family group then went on to Habana and Mavis and I stayed to join in the May Day celebrations.

In 2013 we went for our 50th wedding anniversary, staying mainly in Havana, with a few days in Vinales. It was great a holiday and we stayed with a lovely family, Lourdes and Maykel, who treated us like their grandparents. Our accommodation was recommended to us by our friend, Luis Macarno, a paediatric heart surgeon. Maykel met us at the airport and when I asked how he knew Luis he replied, "Oh, Luis operated on my daughter when she was 6 weeks old, and we have been friends ever since." Can you imagine that happening in Britain? Here is another interesting story about Luis. On one trip I had taken the books The Motorcycle Diaries and Travelling with Che Guevara by his travelling comrade Alberto Granado. When Luis saw the latter book he said, "Alberto is my neighbor, I will get him to sign the book for you."

This year we planned our most adventurous trip ever. We decided to have four weeks there, almost as silver back packers, to celebrate my 75th birthday. I had always said that I would not go to Varadero, having been told it was not the real Cuba. Mavis, who does all our bookings, found that the best prices were flying in and out of this resort town, so that is what we did. We only booked two places to stay, a casa in Varadero and the Havana Libre for May Day. It goes to show that you should not always believe what other people tell you because I thoroughly enjoyed Varadero, staying at Casa Jorge and having a German couple as neighbours. The mosquitos were a problem but then again they find me wherever I go abroad. When Jorge, our host, took our passports to register us he noticed that it was my birthday, so when he brought the passports back he also brought a bottle of wine as a present. We stayed for three nights in this casa and our next stop was Santa Clara. We made a booking by telephoning a casa that we had read about in the Lonely Planet. We had planned to travel there by Viazul coach but were talked into taking a taxi, which was a good choice for a three-hour journey.
We had been to Santa Clara a few years previously, but only for one day, so we looked forward to our return and spending more time at the Che monument, the Che Railway Museum and other attractions. Our accommodation was very good - an old colonial building with very up-to-date facilities. Our host, Pino, the son of the owners of the casa, worked in Italy in Cuba's quiet season and had brought back many items to improve the casa. Pino had also worked in America and Mexico. We stayed there for three nights and when we left Pino took us to the Viazul coach station in his immaculate 1958 Chevy.

Our next destination was Trinidad. Pino had recommended a casa, which he telephoned and booked for us. The owner Irian agreed to meet us at the bus station there. When we arrived our luggage was tied to a bicitaxi and we were transferred to our casa and greeted by all the family. Irian's wife Lilly and daughters Maria and Erica made us feel very welcome. We had been to Trinidad previously and found it to be a wonderful town, but this time it was totally different from our visit five years previously. Now there are lots of casa particulars, shops, cafés and restaurants. Interestingly, many Cuban towns now have a Beatles bar and in Habana there is a Princess Diana Park. We had a great time during our stay, which included a day at Playa Ancon for a swim in the Caribbean sea. There was a Cuban family next to us on the beach who asked us for sun cream, which we gave to them. They then wanted to take photos of us and were very friendly. We stayed with Irian and Lilly an extra night, four in total.

We had planned that Cienfuegos would be our next stop but decided that as we had been there previously we should go instead to Sancti Spiritus, a town we had never visited before. This change of plan proved to be good; Sancti Spiritus is a small town so we saw most of the listed attractions, some very interesting museums and theatres, etc. Even though one theatre was closed the woman in charge allowed us in and gave us a very detailed tour in Spanish, much of which we unfortunately didn't understand.

From here we travelled by bus to Habana as we wanted to be there for the May Day celebrations. The trip took just over 5 hours during stormy weather. Upon arriving in the city we were told that there had been flooding and three people had sadly died as a result.

The Habana Libre was our bit of luxury on the trip. We stayed on floor 22, the one that Fidel used on his victorious arrival in Habana in 1959. We participated in the May Day celebrations in Revolution Square in the rain. We also met Cuban friends whom we had not seen for almost 10 years.

From the Habana Libre, we moved on to stay with Lourdes and Maykel and their two children, Angelica and Marco, whom we had stayed with in 2013. We love Havana and do not get fed up of just wandering the streets discovering new bars and cafes, etc. On this occasion we visited Pepito's Hairdressing Museum, which is a working hairdressers and fantastic. Here I had my haircut - a bit of pampering for me! Whilst talking to Pepito we learned that he ran a free hairdressing school for local young people.

Our next move was to the coast and Gran Caribe Club Atlantic, which was a short taxi ride from Habana. Friends from Britain were there and we had four days relaxing by the sea with them. On our way back to Varadero we stayed at the Hostal Azul, another old colonial house run by a very friendly family. We visited museums, art galleries and the magnificent library. During our stay it was the Cuban Mother's Day, which they take very seriously. It was very pleasing to see people walking through the streets carrying huge cakes on their way to visit their mothers.

Our last stop in Varadero was at the Casa Papo, a more modern house with an equally friendly family. One day we were invited to the birthday party of the owner of the house; they had family there from Spain.

During our four weeks in Cuba we stayed in nine different accommodations, met people from Australia (originally from West Yorkshire), France, America, Germany and Canada. All in all it was a very enjoyable holiday - the best of our many holidays in Cuba.

Index

13732253R00104

Printed in Great Britain
by Amazon.co.uk, Ltd.,
Marston Gate.